Foal to First Ridden

This book is to be returned on or before the date stamped below.

FOAL TO FIRST RIDDEN

A COMMON SENSE APPROACH
TO BREEDING AND TRAINING A FOAL

VANESSA BRITTON

The Crowood Press

First published in 1998 by
The Crowood Press Ltd
Ramsbury, Marlborough
Wiltshire SN8 2HR

British Library Cataloguing-in-Publication Data

A catalogue record for this book is available from the British Library.

ISBN 1 85223 939 5

Line-drawings by Ken O'Brien

Typeset by Phoenix Typesetting, Ilkley, West Yorkshire

Printed and bound in Great Britain by WBC Book Manufacturers Ltd, Mid Glamorgan

Contents

Introduction

WHY BREED A HORSE OF YOUR OWN?

Having embarked upon a long and arduous journey – one that will have taken up more time and money than you ever imagined – what could make up for the endless sleepless nights, the empty bank account and all the hassle and worry along the way? The answer is simple: the reward of a beautiful foal.

However, before you decide to plunge headlong into breeding a foal you must look at why you want one. Putting a favourite mare in foal, even though she has vices and an uncertain temperament, simply to avoid making the decision to sell or retire her is asking for trouble. However, providing you will have a use for the foal, there is much to recommend breeding from a favourite mare if she is sound, viceless and good tempered. Often this is a great way of replacing an older horse with another of similar character and attributes.

It goes without saying that breeding a foal bears a huge responsibility. You must ask yourself if having a foal is something you will be able to follow through for the next few years. Foals are boisterous and need a lot of careful handling; are you sure you have the facilities, time and patience to teach a young horse? You may choose, or circumstances may compel you, to sell the foal on at a later date, but no one wants

a disobedient and headstrong youngster, so make sure you know what is involved in educating a young horse. Having put your mare in foal, it would be unfair to decide you could not cope after the foal is born. There are many horses for sale, but owing to their breeder's lack of knowledge or sense of responsibility many have poor conformation, no ability, or are simply ill-mannered. Therefore, the main caution to breeding your own foal is 'Don't add to this pile of unwanted horses'.

This book will help you to decide not only if your mare is worth breeding from and how to go about doing so if she is, but how to select a suitable stallion and how to care for both mare and foal before, during and after birth. However, before you read the rest of this book take a look at the following points in favour of, and against, breeding, and then ask yourself 'Should I breed from my mare?'

In favour

- Breeding from your own mare is very satisfying, and there is something special in having a son or daughter to follow on from her.
- You can develop a unique bond with a homebred foal from the minute it is born.
- You will be starting with a blank page: there will be no spoilt horse to retrain.
- There will be no uncertain history, or

nasty surprises, as you will know all that has happened to the youngster.
• Breeding a foal is certainly not a cheap option, but if you have a mare capable of breeding an able competition horse it is usually cheaper than buying a 'ready-made' one.
• You can build on your mare's strengths and try to eradicate her bad points by carefully matching her with a suitable stallion.
• Apart from having a horse to ride and train at the end of it, watching a foal being born and growing up is a truly marvellous experience.

Against

• Insufficient knowledge: do you have the expertise to breed and care for a foal? Or do you have someone on hand who does?
• Insufficient facilities: you must have a large enough foaling box, secure fields and safe fencing.
• Breeding, caring for, and training a foal is extremely time-consuming: do you have the time and the patience?

• Your mare will be out of use for nearly two years.
• Finding the right stallion may not be as straightforward as you think: have you the time and the knowledge to make a good choice?
• You are starting with a blank page: all mistakes will be your own.
• Expense: breeding a foal is not a cheap option.
• The nutrition of both the in-foal mare and the foal needs knowledgeable attention.
• You will not be able to ride your foal for at least three years and then it will need expert training for which you will have to pay if you do not have the necessary knowledge and skill.
• You will need suitable facilities for weaning, or will have to pay for either mare of foal to go away for at least three months, ideally six.

As you can see there are more points against breeding than for it, but if you really want to breed a foal, and you are willing to accept the cons with the pros, good luck and read on . . .

1 Assessing Your Mare

Foals inherit and learn a great deal from their mothers, and just as they may acquire her good qualities, they may also develop her bad ones. Therefore, the very first thing to ask yourself is: *'Is my mare worth breeding from?'* The answer is not easy, because there are simply no guarantees of the type of foal a mare will produce. You can match a mare and stallion of excellent conformation and get a foal that looks like a donkey. Similarly, you can match a mare and stallion of apparently poor conformation and get a super foal. However, such cases are usually exceptions to good breeding practice, and it follows that in order to breed a good sound foal, you should aim only to breed from good sound horses. Before you even think of looking for a stallion for your mare you need to assess her attributes and consider how they may influence her foal. The most significant qualities, in order of importance, are:

1. Temperament.
2. Conformation.
3. Action.
4. Ability.

TEMPERAMENT

A good temperament is essential. While a foal's genetic make-up will comprise 50 per cent from its dam and 50 per cent from its sire, it will be in the company of its dam

for six months or so until it is weaned and will therefore learn much of its behaviour from her. In order to be worth breeding from, your mare must enjoy the company of humans and other horses, and be a willing and obedient type; but in particular she should *not* be an aggressive,

Fig. 1 A good temperament is essential in a broodmare. This mare has a large, kind eye and an interested, cheerful expression reflecting her lovely temperament, which has been passed on to her foals.

9

jealous, or skittish sort. From its dam a foal can acquire its attitude towards humans and other horses. It can also learn a multitude of other behavioural traits; such as allowing itself to be caught easily and standing still for the farrier, or trying to nip or kick everything on two legs!

While you will know your own mare's current disposition, try to remember back to her younger days, if you owned her at that time. Was she a cheeky youngster who tried it on at every given opportunity? Or was she a fairly laid-back sort? Was she easy to train when it came to leading, rugging up, catching, clipping and shoeing? Was she easy to back and ride?

Fig. 2 Mares who have a disagreeable temperament should not be bred from, as the resulting foal may display a similar character – regardless of the stallion's temperament.

Did she learn quickly? Or did you have to keep repeating exercises until it all 'sank in'? While there are no assurances that your foal will follow a similar pattern, there is a good chance that it will have the same sort of character. This will give you some idea of what you may expect from the foal both in the short and long term.

CONFORMATION

There are two factors to consider here. Firstly you need to look at the mare's general conformation, and then you need to assess her 'broodmare physique'. General conformation is the physical appearance of the horse, which is determined by the arrangement of muscle, bone and other body tissue. This means the body parts are put together in the proper proportions and dimensions with their correct relations well formed on one another, making the whole structure of the horse symmetrical and sound. If you are unsure how to assess conformation then you should ask the opinion of a knowledgeable friend. No two horses are the same, but nevertheless there are certain desirable characteristics to look for. The following offers a brief guide:

Head
The head should be intelligent with a broad forehead and a large, kind eye. It should be in proportion to the rest of the body with large, well-defined nostrils. The lower teeth should meet the upper teeth squarely. In addition the head should be well set on to the neck with plenty of breathing space between the lower jawbones near the throat.

Fig. 3 A mare with good general conformation. Such a mare is more likely to produce a foal that also has good conformation.

Neck and Shoulder

The neck should be straight or slightly arched, and its length should be in proportion to the rest of the body; not too thick set, nor too weak. The shoulder should be long and sloping from the withers to the point of the shoulder. Such a horse will be a more comfortable ride, as a short, upright shoulder produces a shorter stride.

Back and Withers

The back should be short and strong, neither dipped nor too wide. However, remember that whilst a long back is undesirable, a good broodmare must have sufficient length to accommodate her foal comfortably; she will therefore be longer in the back than her male counterpart. The withers should be prominent, but not too 'cresty', gently tapering away into the back.

Hindquarters

The hindquarters should be straight, strong and broad, reaching well down into the second thigh.

Chest and Girth

The chest should not be too narrow as this will bring the forelegs closer together making the horse move too close in-front. The girth should be deep, and the ribs well sprung.

11

Legs

The forearm should be strong with plenty of muscle. The knees need to be broad and flat to take the weight of the body, and evenly placed so that the bone of the forearm and the cannon bone form a straight line. The cannon bone should be strong and short with clearly defined tendons behind. The amount of bone a horse has is determined by measurement of the whole of the lower limb region just below the knee.

The hind thighs should be long, well muscled and well let down, with the second thigh (gaskin) also strong. Hocks should be large and fairly square, with the point of the hock well defined.

Pasterns and Feet

The pasterns should be sloping and set at a gentle angle. Upright pasterns prevent the buffering of concussion on the joints, and pasterns that are too sloping allow strain to be taken on the suspensory ligament and tendons. The feet should be deep with adequate room between the heels, as narrow boxy feet can restrict the function of the foot. The frog should be firm and well developed, with a shallow depression in the centre.

Naturally, there must be some scope for variation in the above points, as there is no such thing as a horse with absolutely perfect conformation. However, a mare being selected for breeding should possess most of these qualities. Obviously, certain breeds and 'types' of horse can vary considerably in conformation, so what might not be ideal in a dressage horse might be perfectly acceptable in a horse destined for another sphere of equestrianism.

Making a judgement

To enable you to judge conformation correctly you need first to see your mare standing up on level ground. She should not be resting a hind leg, nor have her head held tightly by a handler as this will prejudice the overall picture. Immediately ask yourself, what is your initial impression? Is there anything that directly hits you as being odd, or very nice? Does her head look too small? Does it look intelligent? Does she look strung out, or compact? Are her hind legs underneath her, or still trying to catch up from last week? Does she look symmetrical all over? And so on . . .

In general a 'good' mare will look as though all her pieces flow into one another without any obvious lumps and bumps. In your mind's eye you should be able to draw a square from her withers to her forefeet, along the ground to the hind feet, and up to the croup. Once you have developed an overall impression, start to study specific points of her conformation more closely, as previously described.

Broodmare physique

A good 'broodmare physique' is simply that which will enable her to carry and give birth to a good-sized foal without complications. Try not to be affected by the condition of your mare: whether fat or thin, she is the same underneath, but fat does hide plenty of imperfections if you do not know what to look for. Ideally your mare should have a wide front and a good depth of girth. A short back will not prevent a mare from breeding, but generally mares with longer backs tend to carry foals more comfortably. Any problems you

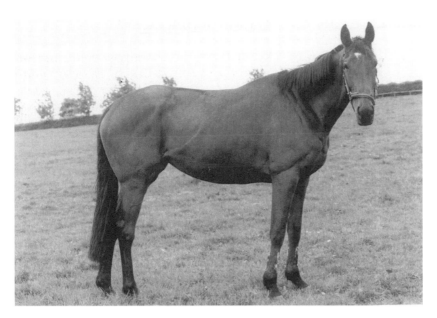

Fig. 4 A mare with pretty awful conformation, and yet she was sent to stud by her owner. While she might produce a nice enough foal, the chances of her doing so are less than those of a mare with good conformation.

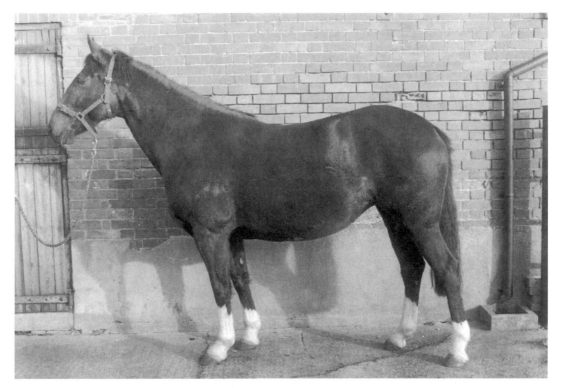

Fig. 5 Generally, mares with longer backs do tend to carry foals more comfortably.

13

have experienced should be checked by the veterinary surgeon to make sure they are not hereditary. Although bad conformation may not have affected your mare's health, if passed on to her foal it may predispose it to all sorts of complications.

ACTION

A mare with good conformation is likely to have a good action and thus desirable paces. However, action does vary between breeds and types of horses. For example, a hack or hunter should move fairly close to the ground with long, free and easy strides. A native pony, such as a Welsh pony will have more knee action, and a gaited horse such as a Hackney will have a high knee action. Whatever the 'typical' action of the breed or type, all paces should be straight, active and rhythmic, with equal stride lengths. It is desirable to watch your mare loose in the field, as then you can assess her paces unrestrained by either rider or handler. Having assessed your mare loose, ask a friend to trot her straight towards you and then past you on a level surface. Does she move straight? Are her strides free and easy? Does she brush, dish or forge? A mare with 'true' action will have her hind legs exactly following her forelegs. When a horse with this true action trots towards you it looks as though she has no hind legs, so squarely do they follow up the forelegs.

ABILITY

Having decided your mare is likely to make a suitable mother, you need to consider her capability to produce what you want. Contemplate the sort of horse you would like: what size, type, ability, and so on. If your aim is to produce an event horse, and yet your mare always received poor marks in dressage and knocked every showjump flying then, regardless of the stallion you choose, you are unlikely to succeed. Similarly, if you want to breed a show horse but your mare has all the charisma of a camel you are likely to be disappointed, however beautiful the stallion. Conversely, if your mare has real looks or talent, and you choose a well-matched stallion you could breed a real winner. While technically a foal takes on 50 per cent of each of its parents attributes, in practice the mare does seem to be more dominant when it comes to ability.

Ideally your mare should have proved herself in the area that you are interested in breeding a foal for. If you want a dressage horse then paces and action will be extremely important. Similarly, if you want to breed a good, safe hack then your mare should have proved excellent in traffic and generally well mannered whenever ridden. There is a lot of truth in the old saying that 'like breeds like'.

AGE

A mare that is too old and stiff to be competed or even ridden is too old to breed from. Putting a mare in foal is not a retirement option, as it puts strain on her musculoskeletal structure as well as her internal systems. Towards the end of pregnancy, a foal can weigh nearly a third of the mare's weight, which undoubtedly puts stress on her back and legs. This is not to say that older mares should not be considered for breeding, but they must be fit and in good condition. Although a lot

14

Fig. 6 If your mare has real looks, and you choose a well-matched stallion, you could breed a winner. This three-year-old was bred from sound parents, did very well in the show ring, and is now a broodmare herself, producing quality offspring.

depends upon the individual mare, an older mare may prove more difficult to get in foal, especially if she is a maiden (a mare that has not had a foal before). A rough guideline is that maiden mares are most likely to have a smooth pregnancy from conception to foaling when they are between the ages of three and fourteen years. Many mares will naturally cease breeding from the age of about fifteen, although mares well in to their twenties have still conceived. The decision must be yours, but do have your veterinary surgeon examine your mare before breeding. If in his opinion your mare is not suitable to breed a foal then take his advice.

PRE-BREEDING HEALTH CHECKS

Having decided that your mare appears to be a suitable candidate for breeding you should have your veterinary surgeon give her a pre-breeding health check, as there are certain things you cannot determine or that will not be obvious to you simply from looking at her. For example, he will check to ensure that her heart, lungs and eyes are sound. If they are not you should not breed from her, as you will be risking not only her life but the life of the foal. Your veterinary surgeon should also check that your mare's reproductive organs are in

Fig. 7 Ideally your mare should have proved herself in the sphere you are interested in breeding a foal for.

good order. Depending upon the time of year, and the stage of your mare's reproductive cycle, he may also be able to give you an idea of how near she is to ovulating (releasing an egg, *see* Chapter 2). In any case he will be able to assess the tone and size of her ovaries and uterus to ensure they are normal. He will also be able to determine if your mare's pelvic girdle is sufficiently spacious to allow the safe passage of a large foal.

HEREDITY

Soundness is a major hereditary factor. In breeding terms, soundness relates not only to the limbs and feet, but to the whole make-up of the horse. Thus an undershot jaw is just as much an 'unsoundness' as a sprained tendon. An unsoundness may be directly inherited from one or other parent; flat feet or a parrot mouth are examples. Or the conformational defect that caused a weakness in the parent may

be inherited, predisposing the foal to the same disorder. As an example, let us take a racehorse with long, light cannon bones. The racehorse is a mare and she breaks down (sprains her tendon) during training. She is mated with a stallion who has average cannon bones. The resulting foal looks like having average cannon bones and stands up to training. However, a few months into its career, when the stress of racing takes hold, it too breaks down. There is a chance that the foal might have stood up perfectly well to racing, but it was undoubtedly a gamble and illustrates why it is important for breeders to select only those mares and stallions that have good conformation.

The most common defects known to be hereditary include:

• Overshot and undershot jaw; parrot- and bulldog mouth.
• Ewe and cresty neck.
• Long or light cannon bones; over-sloping or short upright pasterns; bow,

cow or over-straight hocks; back at the knee.
• Unmatched feet (unless this has occurred as a result of an accident); flat, shallow or weak hooves.
• Sway or roach back.
• Failure of the testes to descend; nymphomania (constant rejection of a stallion even though the mare appears receptive, or not holding to a stallion when mated); pneunovagina (poor conformation of the vagina which then allows air and dirt to enter, requiring a caslick operation if the mare is to be used for breeding – *see* Chapter 8.
• Roaring; dust allergies.

Other allergies and system disorders can also be inherited, as can a sensitivity to environmental factors, so long before you breed from your mare you should take a good overall look at her. As hard as it might seem, you may have to decide against breeding from her and perhaps opt to buy a weanling instead.

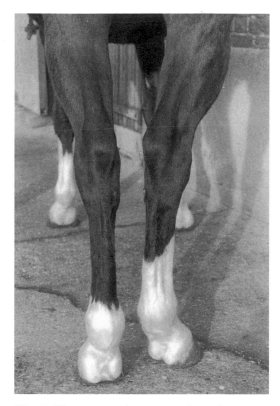

Fig. 8 Most unsoundnesses, such as these cow hocks, are inherited.

Broodmare Checklist
Qualities/Characteristics
• A good temperament
• Correct conformation
• Good movement
• Soundness
• Proven ability
• Intelligence
• Good pedigree
• Good example of type/breed
• Breeding physique
• Successful breeding history
• Keeps in good condition
• Suitable breeding age

By giving your mare a mark out of ten for each of the listed factors, you can appraise her strengths and weaknesses and thus evaluate her suitability as a broodmare. This checklist will also help in your search to find a suitable stallion as you will be looking to find one that scores highly out of ten for any of the factors where your mare's score is low. In this way you can aim to improve on your mare's faults and produce a strong, sound foal.

2 Genetics and Reproduction

Before you can go about choosing a suitable stallion for your mare, you must first have at least a basic idea of how characteristics are inherited. You will then be better able to judge which of a potential sire's attributes are likely to show in his offspring. Genetics is a complex science – one that is beyond the scope of this book – but the following will serve as a brief introduction to the subject.

BASIC PRINCIPLES OF INHERITANCE

Genetics is the science of heredity: the variation of inherited characteristics. The 'building blocks' of genetics are genes. The genes are carried on chromosomes. The horse has 32 pairs of chromosomes, which together dictate everything from the animal's sex to its colour, even the texture of the horse's mane and tail. Each characteristic of the foal is made up from a pair of genes, one gene inherited from its dam and one from its sire. Some characteristics are governed by simple genes but most are controlled by a complex interaction of many genes. An individual horse's total genic make-up is called his genotype.

While a foal receives genes from each of its parents, some of them are dominant and others recessive. A dominant gene will overpower a recessive one, and so the dominant gene's characteristic will show in the foal. The recessive gene will still be there but it will not be manifested in the horse's appearance. Dominance can occur for almost any characteristic.

The second aspect of genetics that has a significance for breeders is the law of 'segregation of genes'. Put simply, this means that while a dominant gene will always show in the first generation, its recessive counterpart may become apparent in the next generation, according to an arithmetical ratio of 3:1, which does not alter. In order to demonstrate this, we can look at the way in which a simple characteristic such as coat colour is inherited. A horse that inherits from each parent a gene for grey colouring is pure bred for grey because he can pass only grey to his progeny; such a horse is known as homozygous (for grey colouring). A horse that has inherited genes for more than one colour – one grey (dominant) and one chestnut (recessive) – will be grey, but since he may pass on either colour to his progeny he is a 'non-true-breeding' grey; such a horse is known as heterozygous. If the homozygous horse is crossed with the heterozygous horse, all their offspring will be grey (since grey is dominant), but they will not all necessarily be homozygous since some of them will have inherited the recessive chestnut gene. If these greys are then crossed, they will produce a ratio of three greys to one chestnut. (This chestnut foal will have inherited a recessive chestnut gene from each parent; the others will have inherited either two grey genes, or one grey and one chestnut.)

Genetics has had a profound effect on horse breeding over the centuries. We can take the British Thoroughbred as a good example. This 'breed' is descended from only three original stallions and a group of about fifty foundation mares, in order to breed in the required dominant genes.

What significance does this have for the amateur breeder?

As we have seen, a horse's genotype is not completely visually obvious since some

of his genetic make-up will be masked by the dominant genes. Those characteristics that are visible and measurable are known as his phenotype and it is this that we judge when we consider a horse's potential. So although a stallion may appear 'physically' to be all you require for your mare, he may be carrying genes that you will find undesirable were they to show in your foal. So an important thing to establish when choosing a sire is whether he 'stamps' his progeny. To do this you must view as many of his foals as possible. Can you clearly see that he has sired them, or are they so different as to prove that he is not a very dominant sire?

If you are lucky you will get a foal that has taken on the best points of both parents and none of the poorer ones. In the past when this happened old 'nagsmen' used to say the mare had 'nicked' with the

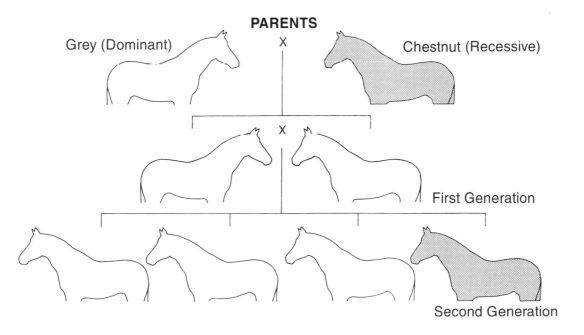

Fig. 9 Segregation of colour genes according to an arithmetical ratio of 3:1.

stallion. In such a case it is a good idea to breed more foals from the same pairing.

The foal's sex

The chromosomes that determine sex are known as X and Y. Your mare will have two X chromosomes, while the stallion has an X and a Y: 50 per cent of his sperm contains X chromosomes while the other 50 per cent contains Y chromosomes; your mare's eggs will all contain X chromosomes. It is therefore the stallion that determines the sex of the foal since he will contribute either an X or a Y to its make-up; the mare can contribute only an X. If the sperm that fertilizes the egg is carrying an X chromosome your foal will be female; if it is carrying a Y chromosome it will be male. It is as simple as that! (*see* figure 10).

Breeding for colour

As we have already seen, colour is something that is inherited from both parents, and if one of the genes inherited from either parent is dominant, this gene will show in the foal's colour. The other recessive gene will still be there, but only becomes important if the foal is bred from.

There are two basic colours in horses: black and chestnut. All other colours are variations of these two, controlled by other colour genes inherited. The dominant gene is black, so if this gene is present in your foal he will be either bay, brown or black. The recessive gene is chestnut, which may or may not be apparent depending on whether it has been masked by a dominant black. As discussed earlier, a chestnut horse can pass on only chestnut genes. Therefore the mating of a chestnut mare with a chestnut stallion can only produce

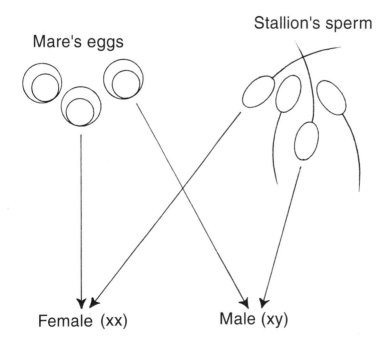

Fig. 10 Determination of a foal's sex.

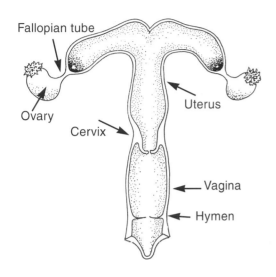

Fig. 11 Reproductive organs of the mare (internal view from above).

a chestnut foal. However, chestnut foals can still result from non-chestnut parents if each parent is carrying a chestnut gene. Similarly, to produce a grey foal, the sire or dam must be grey itself. Grey is an odd colour. The grey gene is dominant, but foals are never born grey. They are born dark, and will continue to lose their colour until they appear grey, or even white. This is why even the darkest dapple or steel grey will eventually turn white.

Colour genes are linked to certain breeds. For instance, Thoroughbreds and Arabs have only black, chestnut or grey genes, while the pure Cleveland Bay horses will produce only bays.

However, that's as simple as it gets! The picture becomes further complicated with 'extra' genes, that come in to produce colour variations such as skewbald, piebald and roan. A skewbald horse will have inherited a gene for white patches and likewise a piebald, with the underlying colour brown or black respectively. A roan has a gene for 'mixed white', whereby white hairs are distributed throughout the basic colour. Other genes have a weakening, or 'diluting' effect. For instance, a chestnut can be weakened to become a palomino, a bay to a dun and if two of these weakening genes are inherited the effect is a cremello or perlino. Appaloosa spotting is caused by a different gene from either piebald or skewbald. Its gene causes mottling of the skin and can also cause striped feet. So, as you can see, unless you are crossing two chestnut parents there are simply no sureties.

THE MARE'S REPRODUCTIVE ORGANS

There is quite a lot to know about the mare's reproductive system and you will find that stud managers, vets and other breeders do not have the time, or the inclination, to use layman's terms. This can cause confusion if you do not understand what is being discussed, so here follows a brief overview.

Your mare's reproductive organs are accommodated to the rear of her abdomen. Broad ligaments attach the cervix, uterus, ovaries and oviducts to the upper body wall. While providing this support, these ligaments also carry the blood, nerve and lymphatic supplies to these organs. The vulva, vagina and uterus form a Y-shaped structure.

Ovaries

The ovaries contain the mare's eggs – the female germ cells, called ova. Unlike sperm, eggs are not produced throughout the mare's lifetime; instead huge numbers are present in the ovaries at birth, where they remain until reproductive maturity is reached and the mare's seasons commence. The main purpose of the ovaries is to control the development – and eventually the release – of an egg (ovum) into the fallopian tube (oviduct) down which it travels in readiness for fertilization. At various points in the mare's cycle, the ovaries also release the hormones oestrogen, progesterone and inhibin. During the spring, the mare's ovaries double in size and become fairly soft, which indicates the development of the follicles (*see* below) and the onset of oestrus (the season). During the winter months the ovaries are small and quite hard, indicating the inactive period of the cycle, known as dioestrus. These changes in the ovaries are detectable on internal examination, enabling a veterinary surgeon to determine your mare's readiness for breeding.

Follicles

A follicle is a fluid-filled sac which contains the ovum and nourishes it after fertilization. Just before and during oestrus, the follicles release oestrogen and start to develop and enlarge. However, there is usually just one that outgrows the rest. This will continue to grow until it is mature, by which time it is referred to as a 'ripe' follicle and you may often hear your veterinary surgeon, or stud manager, referring to this.

Fallopian tubes (oviducts)

These extend from the ovaries to the uterine 'horns'. They act as transportation tubes for both the egg and the sperm and it is here that fertilization of the ovum occurs.

Uterus

The fallopian tubes widen into the uterus, a muscular, tubular organ which ends in the cervix: the opening through which the sperm pass to meet the descending egg. When the fertilized ovum reaches the uterus, it attaches itself to the uterine wall and begins its development into a foal. The mare's uterus is a remarkable structure, capable of self-cleaning should any contamination during mating occur, and of swift recovery from damage during foaling.

Cervix

This is a type of 'valve' between the vagina and the uterus. While it is capable of exceptional relaxation during mating (to accommodate the stallion's penis), and during foaling (to allow the passage of the foal), at all other times it must remain tightly closed so as to prevent infection and offer protection to the foetus.

OVULATION

Ovulation occurs about twenty-four hours before the end of oestrus: the ripe follicle ruptures, releasing the ovum into the open ends of the fallopian tube. After the ovum has left the ovary, the ruptured follicle begins to develop into a structure known as a *corpus luteum*, which begins to produce progesterone. The manufacture of progesterone signals the beginning of

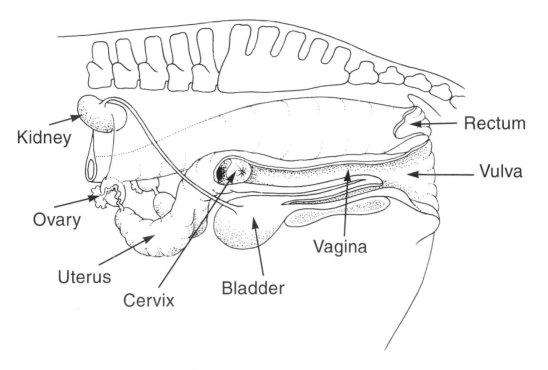

Fig. 12 Reproductive organs of the mare (internal side view).

dioestrus, when the mare is 'out of season' and ceases to be receptive to the stallion. If the mare is mated during ovulation, she should conceive and a foetus develop. If not, the *corpus luteum* will die after eight to twelve days. This process alerts the ovaries to the absence of a foetus and the need to produce oestrogen to start the cycle again.

OESTRUS

As already touched upon, the egg-producing stage in the mare's cycle is controlled by the length of daylight. This is why mares do not come into season during the winter months. As the hours of

daylight start to increase, various parts of the brain which govern the action of hormones are stimulated. Hormones are chemical substances that are produced in various part of the body. They are then transported to other parts of the body via the bloodstream where they produce the desired response. Along with oestrogen and progesterone the two hormones that play the greatest part in the breeding cycle are melatonin and Gonadotrophin Releasing Hormone (GnRH). GnRH is responsible for the onset of oestrus in that it stimulates the pituitary gland to produce follicle stimulating hormone (FSH), which triggers growth of the ova. Melatonin is active during the hours of darkness and works to suppress GnRH. As

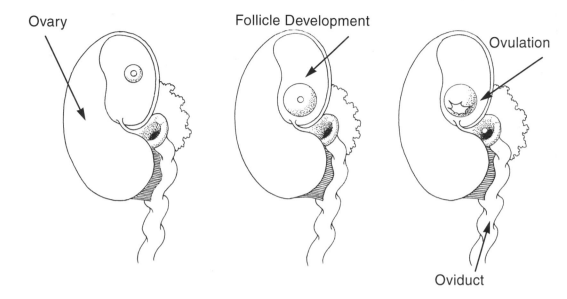

Ovary

Follicle Development

Ovulation

Oviduct

Fig. 13 Stages of ovulation.

the hours of daylight increase in spring, melatonin secretion is reduced. This allows the GnRH to stimulate FSH, and so the mare comes into season. The developing follicles secrete oestrogen, which in turn stimulates the luteal gland to produce Luteinizing Hormone (LH), which encourages the growth and eventual rupture of one follicle.

The usual season lasts around three weeks: five or six days in season (oestrus) and fifteen or sixteen days out of season (dioestrus). This alternating between oestrus and dioestrus continues until the onset of anoestrus in winter, when ovarian activity ceases until a new cycle begins again in the spring. The precise length of oestrus and dioestrus does vary with different horses though, especially as not all mares give outward behavioural signs of being in season. There can also be a considerable variation in the length and character of one mare's cycle as it progresses. At the beginning and end of the breeding season her seasons may appear fairly long and fairly weak, whereas towards the middle they may be shorter and quite intense. If you keep a diary of your mare's dates (when she comes in and goes out of season), this will be very helpful when she goes to the stud.

Behaviour in oestrus

In a very few mares, oestrus has a profound effect on their behaviour. During dioestrus they may behave perfectly well, but once they are in season they can become very uncooperative, even to the point of being simply unmanageable. Maiden mares do occasionally show this behaviour, but those who have produced a foal before seem more susceptible.

Obviously, if a mare conceives she will not come back into season until after the birth of her foal. However, if the mare is not to be bred from her behaviour needs to be controlled. This can happen by giving the mare progesterone, in injection, implant or feed form. This will prevent oestrogen being produced (*see* Ovulation), and thus prevent the mare from coming into season. There is a synthetic form of progesterone called Regumate, which can be given in the mare's feed. This will suppress oestrus while it is being given, but when it is stopped the mare will come back into season (during the spring and summer) about eight days later. Regumate is also used early in the breeding year to induce mares to cycle regularly. An implant – a small tablet inserted beneath the skin – will suppress a mare's season from between six to twelve months.

All of the female sex hormones can easily be measured by taking a blood sample. While abnormal levels do not mean the mare's behaviour will be undesirable, it does help to check that all is normal in respect of her ovaries.

The Breeding Cycle

1. Seasonal/environmental factors trigger hormone activity.
2. FSH stimulates initial ovarian follicle development. Oestrogen levels rise.
3. The mare shows behavioural signs of being in season.
4. The follicles mature to the stage of ovulation.
5. If mated, conception occurs; if not mated, mare starts to go into dioestrus.
6. Fourteen days after ovulation, blood progesterone levels fall, signalling the end of dioestrus.
7. More ovarian follicles start to mature.
8. Another oestrous cycle commences.

3 Selecting the Stallion

When selecting a stallion, choose the best and most suitable stallion within the price range you can afford. For what purpose are you breeding? Does your foal need good solid bone for eventing, a quiet, even temperament for weekend hacking, or a specific profile and bone structure for showing? Once you have decided on the required breed of stallion you should start looking at individual horses. Choosing the cheapest, or the nearest, stallion is simply not an option, unless it so happens (which is highly unlikely) that he is the most complementary to your mare's strengths and weaknesses.

With an experienced stallion who has produced a lot of stock, you will be able to look at his offspring to get a good idea of what he throws. Some stallions throw foals very similar to their type; some may consistently throw big- or small-boned youngsters, or carry a strong colour gene.

Fig. 14 Viewing the stallion's progeny is extremely important. When visiting the stud, you should be able to view foals sired by him, or at least be provided with details of their whereabouts.

While colour is not usually a priority, you may still want to take it into account. Conformation and temperament are far more important, so you must be sure that the stallion is satisfactory in both respects. It is unwise to try to create a bigger horse by choosing a stallion more than two hands bigger than your mare: this will prove to be a futile effort and, worse, you may be inflicting serious problems on your mare, both during covering and throughout the pregnancy.

WHERE TO FIND A STALLION

Individual breed societies are able to supply plenty of information on registered stallions. They are usually extremely helpful and can even supply details about the stallion's appearance, dominant characteristics and successful progeny. General societies in the UK (those not confined to a specific breed) include the National Light Horse Breeding Society, the National Stallion Association, the British Sports Horse Register, and the British Warm-Blood Society, and these will provide details of many stallions of a certain type or breed that might be suitable for your particular mare. Most breed or general societies publish a comprehensive list of all approved and reputable stallions. Many societies have yearly grading and registration days, on which animals come forward to be tested for approval as breeding stock, or 'good examples of the breed'. It is well worth attending these days if the stock is of the breed you are interested in.

Most studs will provide stud cards (and some will now also supply a returnable video) to genuine potential clients; these give essential stallion details and bloodlines. It is also a good idea to go to local shows and stallion parades to see the horses outside their yard environments. Many of the larger studs hold open days early in the year offering mare owners the chance to view many stallions and their progeny in one place.

Once you have made your initial selection of suitable stallions, make appointments to view them at the stud. Apart from allowing you to assess them at closer quarters, this will give you the opportunity to see the standard of horsemanship at the yard, and what facilities are available.

Viewing the stallion

Once you have made your list of stallions to visit, make appointments with each stud to view them. If you are largely unsure of what to look for, take a knowledgeable friend with you. While your main priority is to study the qualities of each stallion, you must also assess the stud itself.

On arrival at the stud, make yourself known to the stud manager. Is he there to greet you? Or are you left waiting before anyone acknowledges your presence? Do the horses appear to be happy and content? Or do they look miserable and discontented? Is the yard clean and tidy? Or are there piles of rubbish laying around? What is the fencing like? Are the beds clean and deep? It does not take long to assess a place and often you will either get a good or a bad feeling about it. Do not be impressed by a lot of technical talk and apparent superiority by the stud manager. If you do not like the stud, do not send your mare to their stallion, however

Fig. 15 On arrival at the stud, study the cleanliness of the yard and the standard of horse management.

much you try to convince yourself it will be tolerable. You will worry the whole time your mare is at stud, and there is no such thing as breeding the 'right' foal at all costs.

ASSESSING A STALLION

When considering any stallion, categorize him according to his:

1. Type.
2. Temperament.
3. Conformation.
4. Ability.
5. Progeny.

Type

Type is the first thing to consider because if it is not right for your mare, it is pointless assessing any other qualities. The stallion's type does not need to be exactly the same as your mare's, but it should complement hers. If you want to breed a pure bred horse then there is no choice: you must choose a Thoroughbred, Hanoverian, Welsh pony, or whatever it is your mare happens to be. However, you may want to cross your mare with another breed to produce a part-bred, perhaps in the hope of producing a foal with more quality, or more bone, than your mare. If you have a Thoroughbred mare, you have quite a lot of options and can mate her with any 'light horse' breed. With draught mares, the choice is either to breed a pure-bred, or to cross with a Thoroughbred to breed in quality. Some breeders do 'experiment', and try other types of stallion with draught mares, but it is my opinion that what is produced certainly does not surpass that of the draught/Thoroughbred cross. Interestingly, a draught stallion to a Thoroughbred mare does not work as well, as the resulting foals tend to be quite heavy and common.

A stocky pony mare of unknown origin can be put to a small Thoroughbred stallion, or an Arab or Anglo-Arab, in order to try to produce a foal that is bigger, and has more quality, than the mare. However, do remember not to choose a stallion that is more than two hands bigger than your mare.

Choosing the right type really comes down to common sense. Assess your mare, then assess the stallion, and try to picture a foal somewhere between the two. If you cannot imagine the result then it probably will not work. If you are really unsure, take with you to the stud a picture of your mare and any pedigree details that you may have. While some stallion owners will tell you that their stallion is ideal, simply because they want the business, most will give you a fair indication of what they feel your mare will produce from their stallion.

As a very 'loose' guide here follows an indication of why you might use a certain breed of stallion:

Cleveland Bay
Originally produced in Yorkshire, this breed was used for farm work, hunting and driving. Good examples of the breed have sired some useful all-round competition horses.

Notable attributes: even temperament, courage, substance and depth of bone. They cross well with Thoroughbred or fine, lightweight mares.

Irish Draught
A native of Ireland, this breed was originally used as an all-purpose horse for farm work and riding. Good all-round stock can be produced from many types of mare, but notably the Thoroughbred, or lighter types.
Notable attributes: depth, substance, calm temperament, adaptability and sure-footedness.

Warmblood
A loose term used to describe European horses of varying origin, including Hanoverian, Trakener, Dutch, Danish, Belgian, Holstein, Selle Francais and Swedish. Most of these European breeds carry Thoroughbred blood, but they do all have individual characteristics to set them apart. On the Continent, stallions have to undergo a vigorous testing and grading process before they are passed for stallion duties. Such horses must show athletic all-round ability and may excel in one or other of the competitive disciplines. They are most popularly crossed with quality British or Irish mares.
Notable attributes: strength, bone, substance, free athletic movement, striking paces, and a docile temperament.

British Native
There are nine in the UK, all of which are excellent types in their own right but which serve as valuable foundation stock for crossbreeding with other types of mare. The larger natives (although they are still ponies) are the Dales, Highland, Fell, Connemara, New Forest, Welsh

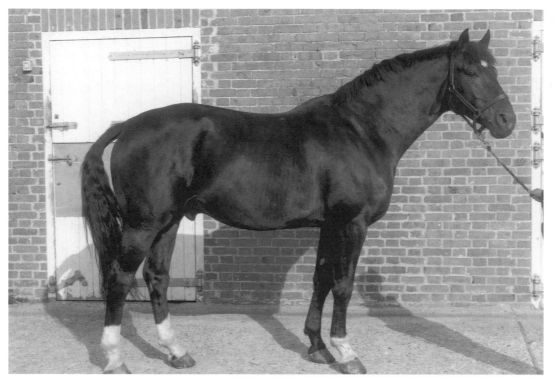

Fig. 16 A Hanoverian stallion that has undergone a vigorous testing and grading process, proving an all-round athletic ability.

Fig. 17 A Shetland pony stallion, one of nine breeds native to the UK, which can all be said to add agility, hardiness and strength to a foal.

ponies of cob type (section C and Welsh cobs), section D and Welsh ponies (section B). The smaller natives encompass the Exmoor, Dartmoor, Shetland and the Welsh Mountain (section A). All natives can be said to add agility, hardiness and strength to a foal. The Welsh Cob/Thoroughbred cross is an extremely popular cross producing some nice-looking, able stock. The result is usually an intelligent, tough, sound horse that is both solid and athletic. A good all-round sort for all the family, usually able to compete in any sphere from eventing to driving. The Connemara cross often produces ideal stock for Pony Club ponies, or if bred with larger horses for smaller competition horses as they are sure-footed, and quick thinking.

Notable attributes: substance, bone, ability and agility, sure-footedness, strength and hardiness. Most also possess a laid-back temperament.

Iberian
The Iberian group includes breeds such as the Andalusian of Spain and the Lusitano of Portugal. These horses are now becoming more popular and offspring can be seen competing in all spheres.

Fig. 18 Arabs can be exceptionally strong, and they are unequalled when it comes to the field of endurance.

31

Notable attributes: very willing temperament, high active paces, presence and solidness.

Quarter Horses

Another breed (originating in the USA) that is increasing in popularity. They are fairly compact, versatile horses that can be crossed successfully well with thoroughbred or natives alike.

Notable attributes: speed, balance, power and agility.

Arabs

An Arab's fine, delicate looks set it apart from any other breed of horse. Arabs are a breed that you either love or hate, and although there are no definite guidelines most are between 14.2hh. and 15hh. There is no such thing as a pony Arab, even if it is under 14.2hh. The most usual cross is with a Thoroughbred to produce an Anglo-Arab.

Notable attributes: their looks belie the fact that they can be exceptionally strong and are unequalled when it comes to endurance.

Be prepared that some studs may not accept your mare if they feel she is not a good breeding candidate. While you might feel a little peeved about this at the time, it is better to find out sooner, rather than later, that your mare is simply not likely to breed a good foal. If it is the draw of a youngster that makes you want to breed, you would be far better buying a weanling.

Temperament

Once you have established that the stallion is a suitable type for your mare, the next thing to assess is temperament. Ask to see the stallion loose in his paddock; however, this is not always possible and your viewing will probably be confined to over the top of the door. Then ask to see him tied up in his box so that you can take a good overall look at him. Some studs may allow you to get close and fuss him, others will not. It is simply a matter of policy, and that a stallion is not allowed to be touched does not mean there is anything wrong with him. While in the box take note of his general attitude. Does he stand still, or is he always fidgeting and pulling on the lead? Does his expression look kind, or menacing?

If you like what you see, ask for him to be led out and trotted up. Once out of his stable does he immediately impress you? You can expect him to be full of charisma, showing a bright, alert and interested character. He may also appear to be a bit of a handful. This is natural. Stallions are an imposing sight when they stand proud so if he does not impress you then he is probably the wrong stallion for your mare. When he is led away, take special notice of his walk. Is it free and easy, or 'stuffy'? When he trots back towards you does he float along the ground, or is his action a little common? Obviously, quite a lot depends on the breed of stallion, but he should instantly inspire you to say, 'yes, this is the one'. If he is nasty, very difficult or fretful, cross him off your list.

Conformation

Provided you are happy with the stallion's temperament you can then go on to assess whether his conformation will complement your mare's. If your mare has exceptionally good conformation the assessment will be a fairly easy one; you

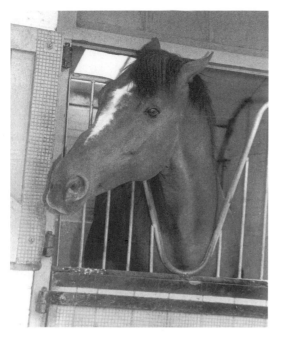

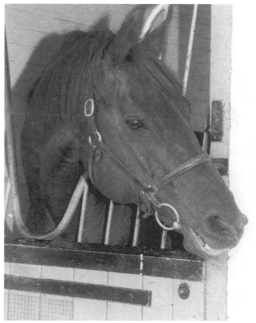

Fig. 19 A good temperament is very important in a stallion. Consider whether he seems temperamental . . .

Fig. 20 . . . or laid-back, yet enthusiastic.

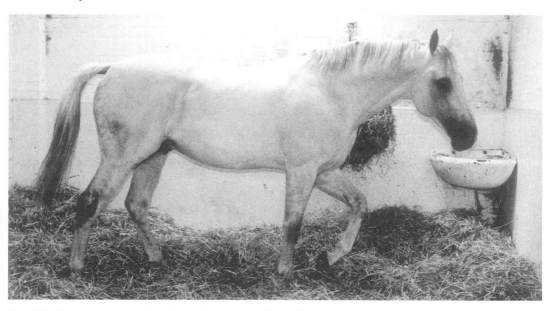

Fig. 21 If viewing is confined to looking over the stable door, watch to see whether the horse is at ease or fretful in the stable.

Fig. 22 Once out of his stable, does the stallion immediately impress you? Or does he fall short of your ideal?

will simply need to establish that basically he has good conformation. However, if your mare has some weak points you will want to see that the stallion definitely does not have the same weak points; in fact you will want them to be his strong points. For instance, if your mare has upright pasterns, the stallions should ideally have good, sloping ones. Similarly, if your mare's hind legs are a little too straight, you will look to see that the stallion's are well proportioned. Likewise you may look at the horse's features. If your mare's head is quite plain you will want to find a stallion with a quality head. This selective process will help to ensure that the resulting foal will have the best possible chance of being a good-looking, well conformed animal. However, as has

been said all along, there are no guarantees, and often quite a few surprises!

Ability

Ability is another important area to consider. Has the stallion competed and retired to stud sound in the discipline that you are looking to breed a foal for? Has he shown an all-round ability, or has he got no form whatsoever?

Progeny

What a stallion produces is actually more important than what he looks like himself. However, rarely does a weak-looking

Fig. 23 If the stallion looks to be an ideal sire for your foal, study his progeny carefully, ideally over a range of ages. Make sure you establish that he 'stamps' his foals.

stallion with lots of faults throw classy foals, so you do have to look at the stallion and his progeny as a 'package'. If a stallion looks to be the ideal sire for your foal, make sure you establish that he 'stamps' his foals as well (*see* page 19).

BREEDING FOR PERFORMANCE

If your sole aim is to breed a horse for a specific type of competition, you must make absolutely certain that the stallion has the required ability in that area (remembering, of course, that your mare must have as well). While the stallion's competitive record will speak for itself, it is useful to have an idea of his way of going

so that you can compare this to your mare's. Unless the stallion is retired from work, you can ask to see him ridden. Take a really good look at him under saddle. Does he still look impressive? Is he all that you expected he would be? If jumping ability is important, ask to see him jumped. Some studs have produced a video of their stallions to prevent the necessity of having him ridden for potential clients. This obviously aids the stud's routine and preserves the stallion's energies, so do not feel you are being palmed off if you are invited to see a video instead.

The stallion owner will be interested to hear about your mare; of any competitive successes that she has had and of her breeding. They will be able to advise, and may even be able to show you, the sort of foals that have been produced from other mares of the same type as yours, put to their stallion. If your mare has proved herself admirably in a certain discipline, the stallion owner may be inclined to offer a concession to encourage you to let her come to their stallion. If the resulting foal does some good, it can only help the stallion's reputation.

Once you have made a decision on your foal's sire, you can discuss terms and procedures. The stud will provide full details of conditions of acceptance, stud, keep charges, and so on. If for any reason they do not, you must ask for them so that you know what the financial implications are from the outset.

Fig. 24 While a stallion's competitive record will speak for itself, it is very useful to have an idea of his way of going so that you can compare it to your mare's.

4 Sending Your Mare to Stud

Studs operate in one of two ways. Studs running for commercial breeders will have their veterinary surgeons take a lot of the guesswork out of breeding. They will have him examine the mare internally and may even have him scan the ovaries in order to determine the optimum date for covering. A blood test may also be taken to measure the hormone levels in the blood in order to be even more precise about the covering date. Such measures do offer mare owners the best chance of getting their mares in foal, which is obviously important when breeding commercially. However, such measures are also costly.

Studs operating for private mare owners operate in a more traditional way. However, this does not mean they are any less professional in their attitude towards the management of mares. They will 'tease' mares with either the stallion to be used, or with an older, less fertile stallion, or with a rig (a gelding that displays stallion behaviour); by gauging a mare's response to the teaser, an experienced handler is able to determine whether ovulation is taking place. They will cover the mare with the stallion when she appears to him in a submissive state and will only involve a veterinary surgeon if there appears to be complications. Such methods still have a good rate of success

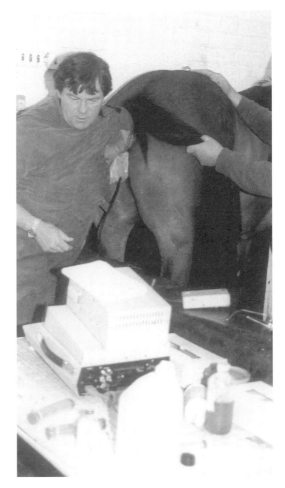

Fig. 25 *Studs operating for commercial breeders have their veterinary surgeon take a lot of the guesswork out of breeding.*

and are less costly than those that rely on a high veterinary involvement.

There are no guarantees that either method will get your mare in foal, but each stud will do its best to ensure it is not for the want of trying. What you must do is to ensure you are happy with the stud's normal practice before you send your mare. Do not be afraid to ask all the questions you want. You are paying for a service, and you are entitled to see just what it is you are getting for your money.

NOMINATION FORMS

Once you have decided upon the stallion to use you should contact the stud who will send you a nomination form. Studs have a maximum number of mares that they allow to any one of their stallions during the breeding season. They also need to try to ensure that mares come in at different times, so that the stallion can physically cover them all. For this reason, it is necessary for each mare owner to send in a nomination form; the stud manager can then plan the stud routine on a weekly basis. By filling in the nomination form you commit your mare to that stallion (you may forfeit a fee if you fail to honour the agreement). The stud is also committed to making sure the stallion is available to cover your mare. Many nomination forms will ask for detailed information about your mare, which might include whether she has any vices or idiosyncrasies that could affect their management of her. For instance, if she is difficult to catch they will need to know so that it does not hinder the breeding programme. They will also ask about health matters relating to breeding, and her general state of health,

which requires you to disclose whether your mare suffers from any condition, such as COPD (Chronic Obstructive Pulmonary Disease).

FEES AND COSTS

Producing a foal from your own favourite mare can be most rewarding, providing years of pleasure and a wealth of experience. There has to be a 'but', of course, and it usually comes in the form of funding. Breeding your own foal will cost you a lot of money; there is no cheap option unless you put your mare at risk. So before any practical arrangements are made, make sure you can afford it.

Obviously if you are going to choose the stallion, the covering fee is to a certain extent down to you. However, the stallion's reputation and the size of the fee are directly related, so a well-respected sire who constantly throws good stock will warrant a high fee. While breeding should not be contemplated merely for profit-making purposes, you should take heart from the fact that the foal's value will be greater accordingly.

The keep of your mare can also mount up, although how long she stays at the stud after pregnancy confirmation, or even after covering, may again be down to you. The fee for the initial veterinary swab before she goes to stud, plus any further veterinary examinations and treatments at the stud, including a pregnancy diagnosis, must also be considered. There is usually a groom's fee, which may be incorporated into the overall charge. Any treatment by the blacksmith, including removal of shoes, should also be taken into account, and in the long term all the foal's costs, like worming, vaccinations and registration. Once you are sure you can afford these costs, you can seriously think about putting your mare in foal.

Terms

Terms and conditions of covering fees vary enormously, so make sure you ask and understand what payment is required, and when, before you fill in the nomination form. It is important that you realize that the 'terms' only cover the stallion's covering fee. The mare's keep and veterinary charges will be extra. The usual terms are:

NFFR
This stands for No Foal Free Return. Should your mare fail to conceive, or lose a foal before full term or have a foal still born then you will be entitled to return the mare to the same stallion to cover her again the following year with no further covering fee (although further keep and veterinary fees will still be incurred).

NFNF
This stands for No Foal No Fee and means exactly what it says: unless your mare produces a live foal there is no fee payable. Obviously, keep and veterinary charges while your mare is at stud are still incurred.

Straight Fee
This means that you pay for the mare to be covered, regardless of whether this results in a pregnancy. It can often be a lower fee, but it is a great risk.

October 1st
This means that provided the mare is tested in-foal on October 1st the covering

fee is due. If the mare is empty then no covering fee is payable. The stud will require sight of the veterinary surgeon's negative pregnancy test results before waiving the fee.

Live Foal
This means the fee is due only if a live foal is born. Often the agreement is that the fee will not be payable if the foal does not survive for more than forty-eight hours, but thereafter (regardless of what happens) the fee is due. This can be a good agreement to make with the stud if you know your mare is very difficult to get into foal, or if she has a history of abortions. They may charge a higher fee overall, but in the long run it will still work out better for you.

Split Fee
This means that half of the covering fee is paid when the mare is tested in-foal (usually scanned at about eighteen days) and the remaining half on October 1st. This can be of benefit if your mare has a history of slipping foals early in her pregnancy, in which case it might be hoped that there will be enough time to cover her again before the end of the breeding season.

PREPARING YOUR MARE FOR STUD

Before the stud will consider using their stallion to cover your mare, they will need to see the results of a clitoral swab to check for a condition known as Contagious Equine Metritis (CEM). This can be done at home by your vet, or at the stud by their vet; your mare does not need to be in season. The test is to check there are no infections in the vulva or genital tract that could harm the stallion if he covers her. The result will be available about seven to ten days after the test, and a veterinary certificate will be required by the stud as proof of the swab results.

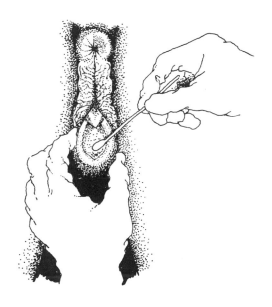

Fig. 26 Clitoral swab.

A cervical/uterine swab (also referred to as an endometrial swab) will need to be taken when your mare is in season. This relates to her gynaecological condition, and will detect any infection or contamination. As the uterus dilates when a mare is in season, to allow passage of the sperm, infection is fairly common. About 8 per cent of mares going to stud will have an infection so do not worry too much if your mare shows to be positive. The vast majority of such infections can be easily and quickly treated by irrigating the uterus with appropriate antibiotics.

On a more general note the stud will expect your mare's vaccinations to be up to date. They will require her to be vaccinated against equine influenza and tetanus, and in some cases against herpes as well.

One last point that few people mention is that it is a good idea to inform your insurance company that your mare has gone to stud. In the unlikely event that she becomes ill, or gets injured, you may find that unless they were given prior knowledge of her whereabouts, she may not be covered.

The last thing you should do is to remove her hind shoes and to make sure she arrives at the stud in a clean, well-fitting headcollar.

CHOOSING THE TIME OF YEAR

The best time for a foal to be born is in the spring. The average pregnancy lasts for just over eleven months, so for an April foal the mare must be sent to stud in May of the previous year. Some studs will take in mares as early as March or as late as August, although for Thoroughbred breeding the official stud season starts on 15 February. It is best to aim for your foal to be born at the time of year when the weather is not too extreme, as your mare and foal will be more comfortable. The grass will contain more goodness in spring and, should you want to show your foal, he will be big and strong by the time the showing season begins. A May foal can be weaned at six months of age in November, which will prevent the mare from being dragged down by the foal over the winter months.

Of course, not all mares will conceive just when we want them to. If your mare should take some time to get in foal do not worry. You may have to take extra precautions during the winter if your foal cannot be weaned, such as extra feed for the mare and foal, and perhaps stabling during harsh weather, but this does not usually cause too many problems. Provided such measures are taken there is no reason why mare or foal should suffer in any way from a late foaling.

If your mare does not conceive straight away, naturally the foaling date will be put back; to allow for this it is a good idea to plan a spring foal so that you have time to have her covered again if necessary.

Your mare may only be covered on one occasion, or daily or every other day for the next week while she is in season. It all depends on stud procedure, and most likely the stud vet's advice after examination of your mare.

THE MARE AT STUD

When a stallion is left to roam with his mares, natural sexual behaviour patterns normally ensure that the mares are covered at the correct time. However, most mares are now covered in-hand at studs. This means it is up to you to present your mare at the correct time, and up to the stud to cover her with the stallion when appropriate. If you are not sure when your mare comes into season you can take her to the stud and leave it up to them to 'try' her each day until she shows she is ready for mating. However, this can work out to be quite costly, so you are better to observe her at home until the time is right. If you have access to a gelding you can 'try' your mare to him, to see if she shows some interest. Try your mare over a fence, or even over her stable door; if you don't have

a barrier between them one or other horse may get hurt if your mare, or the gelding, is not interested. If your mare does not 'show' to the gelding, it does not mean she is not in season. Smell and sight also play a part in the sexual behaviour of mares, so without the presence of a stallion your mare may not show at all even though she is, in fact, ready to be covered. In such circumstances you will either have to take your mare to stud in order for them to tease her with a stallion until ready, or you can have your veterinary surgeon give your mare an internal examination to see if she is in oestrus.

'Showing'

Occasionally, mares have 'silent heats' whereby they show no signs, but if presented to the stallion will accept him. Such mares are best sent to stud in order that the experienced stud staff can interpret subtle signs and have their veterinary surgeon give a clinical opinion on the mare's readiness to be covered.

If your mare is not ready she will quickly reject the stallion. She may be quite hostile towards him. She may swish her tail, flatten her ears back, and may even try to bite or kick him.

If you know your mare well you may detect subtle changes in her behaviour. However, sexual behaviour varies greatly from mare to mare and the modern management of horses can help to disguise such behaviour. The classic signs of a mare 'showing' in season are that she adopts a stance similar to that for urination, but she will stand in this position repeatedly and for lengthy periods with her tail raised. Additionally, she may stay in this 'straddle' position long after she has

Fig. 27 It is quite easy to see when a mare is rejecting the stallion as she may be quite hostile towards him.

urinated. She will also 'wink', by which is meant that she lengthens her vulva and recurrently exposes her clitoris. She will often pass a bright, yellow-coloured urine which contains pheromones (which have a characteristic odour). When in the presence of the stallion, this will stimulate his sexual behaviour and the mare will willingly accept him. Other signs include squealing at other horses in the field, swishing her tail, and being reluctant to move when asked.

Stud procedure

You have sent your mare to stud, but then you begin to wonder what is happening to her. Depending on what you have requested she will either be put into a field with other mares waiting to be covered, or she will be stabled. If she is known to be in season she will be brought before the stallion or teaser to see if she is ready. If she is, she will show the signs as described earlier in this chapter, and the stallion will cover her. If she is not ready she will show that she is not and she will be put back out or into her stable and tried again until she will stand for the stallion.

If the mare is known to be 'difficult' (meaning she will not show or stand for the stallion, even though a veterinary surgeon deems her to be exactly right for mating) then the stud may use artificial means in order to make her stand to be

Fig. 28 A mare showing in season will 'wink'.

Fig. 29 She will also pass a bright-yellow-coloured urine, which contains pheromones.

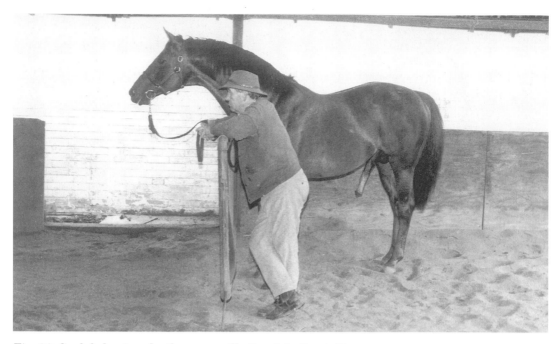

Fig. 30 Such behaviour by the mare will stimulate the stallion.

Fig. 31 Flehmen's posture, classically shown by the stallion in response to an in-season mare.

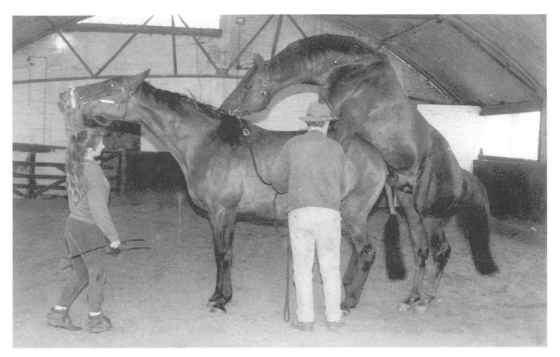

Fig. 32 If the mare shows all the signs of accepting the stallion she will be covered.

covered. These can include the twitch and hobbling. Once the mare has been success-fully covered she will return to the field or stable.

A successful covering should mean that fertilization has taken place. However, this process is not an easy one. It involves complex integration between the repro-ductive organs, their anatomy, function and hormone activity, not to mention the stallion's and mare's own behaviour. So a successful covering does not guarantee that your mare will be in foal.

Anoestrus

Anoestrus is the period of the oestrous cycle when ovarian activity is at its lowest. This naturally occurs in all mares during the winter months, but in some mares it may continue for longer than it should.

In some such cases, the presence of the stallion and the other horses at the stud may encourage your mare to come into season as usual. However, if this does not happen, the stud vet can administer an injection of prostaglandin (also known as PG). This is a hormonal substance that mares produce naturally when in oestrus. It will bring the mare into season within approximately two to four days.

Artificial lighting during the evenings can also be used to exploit your mare's oestrus cycle. Some studs will artificially increase the hours of light available to the mare during late winter and early spring in order to bring the mare into season up to two months earlier than she might naturally do. Other factors such as food availability, the scents given off by mares and stallions (known as pheromones), and the surrounding temperature can also be used to 'kick-start' oestrus.

One of the most significant factors for non-commercial breeders is that of early grass growth associated with good spring weather. A pleasant, early spring will mean mares will become active early in the year, and likewise prolonged harsh conditions can delay the whole stud year.

Artificial Insemination

Artificial Insemination (AI) has its advantages and disadvantages. Firstly, it can help to get a difficult mare in foal. It can also mean that a competition stallion can sire foals without interrupting his competitive career. However, contrary to popular belief it is *not* a more simple or less costly way of getting a mare into foal. Let us consider the reasons that might lead you to conclude that AI would be a good idea for your mare.

1. You want to use a stallion from abroad. While it is possible to send your mare abroad (Thoroughbreds for racing are indeed sent), AI would be a cheaper and less traumatic option for your mare.
2. Your mare does not travel well. A bad traveller may fail to conceive if covered soon afterwards, or may reabsorb on the return journey home, through fretting.
3. Your mare may have sustained an injury that prevents travelling. AI will be the only way of getting her into foal.
4. Your mare may be susceptible to infection of the uterus and may

have been caslicked (stitched). AI prevents the need to unstitch and restitch the mare after covering and thus saves on veterinary fees.

5. Your mare may have a physical problem that means she cannot be covered by the stallion. An example might be a back problem that means she could not bear the weight of the stallion. However, if the condition is a permanent one you should check with your veterinary surgeon that she will be able to carry the weight of the foal without further damage or pain. Of course, if a back problem is caused by a genetic fault the mare should not be bred from in any case.
6. Your mare may have just had a traumatic foaling in which case AI would be a gentler option.
7. Your mare may be the sort that frets all the time she is at stud, and thus is difficult to get into foal. AI is less stressful as the mare does not need to leave her normal surroundings.
8. Your mare may have recently had a weak foal and so it would be unwise to transport it to stud with the mare.
9. You want to use a stallion at a stud that only offers AI (such as when a stallion is competing).
10. Your mare will under no circumstances accept a stallion even though a veterinary surgeon confirms her to be ready for mating.

If one of these reasons leads you to believe that AI is the way forward for your particular mare you should be aware of the procedure. You have to let the stud and your veterinary surgeon know that you want your mare to be inseminated. Only certain studs offer the service so make sure you choose an appropriate stallion. Your veterinary surgeon may not carry out the procedure himself, so you may need to call in a specialist vet. The vessel that transports the semen is called an Equitainer which can cost quite a lot to be delivered. Your mare may only be inseminated once during her season, or twice, and if she does not conceive straight away then you will have to pay again the next time she is in oestrus. In many cases the terms are a straight fee, so whether your mare conceives or not you will have to pay. Just imagine paying your vet to come out four or five times (remember he has to

Fig. 33 As early as eighteen days after service, an ultra-sound scanner can confirm whether or not the mare has conceived.

come out in the first place to establish when your mare is ready to be covered and this may take a few visits if she is not in season when he first calls), then for the Equitainer to be dispatched four times, then to pay the straight fee, and still your mare fails to conceive. You should be aware that the conception rate by AI can be lower than through natural service, so the costs can be quite considerable. On the other hand, you may be lucky and find that you need only two visits by your vet and your mare conceives first time. However, this all points to AI being a bit of a gamble. In your case it may be the only way forward, but only you can decide whether this is so or not.

If you do decide to opt for AI for your mare, let the stud know in plenty of time. They will then send you all the specialist literature on correct procedure. They will also let your veterinary surgeon have the same.

Pregnancy testing

To determine whether your mare is pregnant, the stud vet will perform a pregnancy test. If she does not return into season, there is every likelihood she is pregnant, although proof is required. The most usual method of testing is with an ultrasound scanner at about eighteen days after covering; in addition, manual diagnosis is usually carried out by your vet after forty-five days, as the scanner may no longer be accurate at this stage.

Following a positive pregnancy test, you may want to bring your mare home. You could leave her at stud, although the cost of her keep may dictate your decision. Her well-being must be of paramount importance, so if you consider the stud facilities and security to be better than your own, leave her there.

You have completed the first stage in the breeding process, and if it has gone without a hitch your dream is halfway to becoming a reality. You will probably spend the next eleven months more apprehensive than your mare! For now, though, you can breathe a sigh of relief, and let her encounter the joys of life as a mum to be.

Infertility

The worst possible scenario is that no matter what you or the stud try, your mare fails to conceive. Mares can fail to do

so for either physical or psychological reasons, although most mares do breed quite easily. The only thing you can do in such circumstances is to take a specialist veterinary surgeon's advice. There are extreme measures that can be taken to try to make a mare conceive, but these are immensely costly and not without risk, so they are considered only if the mare is thought likely to produce exceptional foals.

THE STUD YEAR

The following provides a quick-reference guide to what should be happening when:

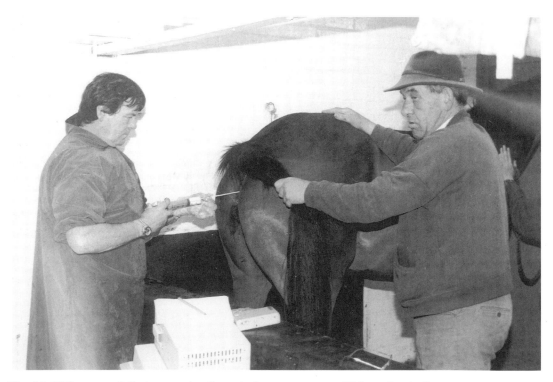

Fig. 34 If the mare fails to conceive the veterinary surgeon will investigate the cause. It may be quite simple, such as an infection which can be treated with drugs, or more serious, in which case the veterinary surgeon will advise on the appropriate action.

Month	Action
January	Health and pre-breeding checks by veterinary surgeon. Overview your facilities and ensure they are suitable. Send for stud cards of suitable stallions.
February	Fix your budget, but allow for some variation. View stallions and stud premises. Ensure mare's condition is neither too fat nor too thin.
March	Discuss all fees likely to be incurred with proposed stud. Reserve the stallion by returning nomination agreement.
April	Have mare swabbed. Observe mare's seasons and record dates. Ensure horsebox is in working order, or arrange transport. Prepare mare for stud: remove shoes, worm and vaccinate as appropriate. Ensure mare's paperwork is in order: ask the stud exactly what they will want to see.
May	Covering in May will produce an April foal. Send mare to stud when due to come into season. Inform stud of your mare's normal routine and feeding requirements.
June	If mare is tested in foal she can return home. Normal routine can resume.
July	Continue normal routine.
August	Continue normal routine.
September	Continue normal routine.
October	Continue normal routine.
November	Ensure strict worming programme is adhered to. Pregnancy can be confirmed by a urine test.
December	Decrease riding to slow paces. Turn mare out for as long as possible.
January	Gradually phase in higher protein feed. If mare is still ridden, only walk.
February	Cease riding altogether. Ensure foaling box is ready and in good repair. Install closed-circuit TV if possible.
March	Make deep straw bed with thick banks in foaling box. Prepare foaling kit. Put mare in foaling box and observe last thing at night and early in the morning.
April	Be prepared for your foal from three weeks prior to the expected date. Check your mare at regular intervals day and night. Constant surveillance once she shows imminent signs or unusual behaviour.
May	Enjoy your foal!

5 The Pregnant Mare

The average gestation period for mares (from conception to birth) is 340 days (eleven months and five days). Routine care of the mare during this time is very similar to that prior to her being in foal. She should be wormed properly (*see* page 53), have her teeth checked every six months, and have her feet trimmed regularly. It is very important to keep a mare's feet in good order. As she becomes heavier they will take more stress, and if they are not trimmed properly they will start to

Fig. 35 An in-foal mare does not need to be 'fed for two' until the last three months of pregnancy. Good grass will provide most, if not all, of her daily requirements.

crack. If her feet seem to suffer quite badly, you may have to keep front shoes on her up until foaling, but they *must* be removed before she foals.

Grooming is also beneficial as it offers a mild massage and helps to keep her muscles toned up. However, the further into the pregnancy your mare gets the more irritable she may become, sometimes to the point of snapping at you. If your mare is obviously not enjoying the attention you are giving her, and she is otherwise healthy, she is best left alone.

FEEDING AND NUTRITION

It follows that a sickly, malnourished mare is unlikely to produce a healthy, well-nourished foal. The mare's body will direct all the nutrition it can to support the foal, even to the point of her own near starvation, but the result will be either a dead mare, and thus foal, or a sickly foal and a very weak mare.

The correct nutrition of a broodmare starts even before she has been covered. A mare is more likely to conceive if she is neither too fat, nor too thin; so getting her into shape is as important before foaling as it is when you are getting her ready to compete.

Once you are happy with her condition, you should ensure that her vitamin and mineral levels are satisfactory. It is a sensible practice to supplement her rations with vitamins and minerals for at least one month prior to, and one month after, covering. However, do not overdo it as you will simply be wasting money. Use a general supplement that offers a bit of everything unless, of course, you know your mare to be deficient in a particular nutrient.

Once your mare is tested in foal you should *not* start 'feeding for two'. Up to about three months before foaling, your mare's nutritional requirements will be as before. She needs feeding in order to maintain her bodyweight, her condition, her body temperature and, if she is being exercised, her workload as well. The foal will require very little on top of this at this early stage, so any increase in feeding will simply result in your mare getting too fat. As a very rough guide your mare will require a 75 per cent forage to 25 per cent concentrate ration, which offers an overall crude protein level of about 10 per cent. One thing you can do is to ensure your mare is provided with a vitaminized and mineralized feedblock. This can be left in the field or stable and she will take what she needs at will. A salt-lick is also beneficial. It is important that you ensure she has enough roughage throughout her pregnancy, so if grass supplies become depleted, you should offer ad-lib hay or alfalfa cubes.

About eight months into the pregnancy you will need to pay more attention to your mare's nutritional needs. This is because the foal starts to grow rapidly at this time: between now and the birth the foal will double in size. Your mare's requirement for protein, calcium, vitamins and minerals now increases, and it is at this point that mare owners start to feel that 'something is happening at last!'

So what extra requirements will your mare have? It is not easy to offer general guidelines as there are all sorts of complicating factors, which are outlined here:

• The foal's due date.
  This has a bearing on feed requirements. A foal due in early April means there will be no lush spring grass for

the mare prior to foaling, but what if the foal is not due until July?

- The breed of the mare.
  If the foal is not due until July, a native pony will need more consideration than a Thoroughbred mare.
- Age of the mare.
  An older mare may need more food than will a younger one in order to support the later stages of pregnancy.

With the above provisos in mind, the following are some guidelines that will help you to assess your individual mare's needs:

- Most horse mares require 12 per cent crude protein from twelve down to six weeks before foaling. To establish the amount of crude protein in any one type of feed, read the analysis label on each bag. If you are still in doubt, most manufacturers have a helpline that you can call.
- At six weeks prior to foaling the crude protein requirement can increase to 14 per cent.
- Native pony mares usually require 20 per cent less crude protein than horses, so they will need about 9.6 per cent crude protein from twelve weeks prior to foaling and 11.2 per cent from six weeks prior to foaling.
- A constant supply of fibre is essential.
- Vitamin, mineral and amino acid levels should be maintained using a broad supplement. If in doubt have your veterinary surgeon take a blood test to check for any deficiencies.
- Fresh spring grass contains a lot of goodness, so concentrate supplementation may need adjusting to allow for this.
- A horse mare's total feed requirement will rise from 2.5 per cent of bodyweight (2.5kg/5lb 8oz per 100kg/220lb of bodyweight) to 3 per cent of bodyweight (3kg/6lb 10oz per 100kg/220lb of bodyweight).
- A pony mare's total feed requirement will rise from 2 per cent of bodyweight (2kg/4lb 6oz per 100kg/220lb of bodyweight) to 2.5 per cent of bodyweight (2.5kg/5lb 8oz per 100kg/220lb of bodyweight).
- Use compound feeds that have already been 'balanced' by the manufacturers, especially those formulated specifically for the breeding industry. If you mix your own 'straights' you can never be sure of their deficiencies, unless, of course, you are a nutritionist.
- Make sure any feed you use is still 'in date'. If not, the vitamins and minerals may have been lost.

Herbal supplements

Raspberry is a commonly used additive at stud as it is known to aid parturition in mares and enhance virility in stallions. The leaves contain fragrine which, when used in the two months prior to foaling and directly after foaling, helps to improve muscle tone and makes for a good milk yield.

Feeding probiotics just before and after foaling will help your mare's system cope with the event and it will also help to prevent scouring. Probiotics are beneficial gut micro-organisms that are normally found in the digestive system.

Other herbal supplements or even homoeopathic remedies may be useful for certain conditions in individual mares, especially as such treatments cannot harm mare or unborn foal. However, it is sensible to consult a well-respected herbalist or a homoeopathic veterinary surgeon, rather than diagnosing and treating your own mare.

Fig. 36 Feeding probiotics prior to and post foaling will help your mare's system cope with the event.

WORMING AND VACCINATIONS

Having already seen how important the correct nutrition of both mare and unborn foal is, you should ensure that nothing jeopardizes the effort you are putting in. Making sure your mare is in good health means ensuring she is also properly wormed and vaccinated. Neither your mare's body, nor her foal's should have to compete with worms for their nutrients.

Every wormer is different so you must follow the manufacturer's instructions when dosing pregnant mares, or check with your veterinary surgeon if you are unsure. Worms present an all-year-round problem for both mare and foal. Some worms are more troublesome than others at various times of the year, but generally if you ensure you follow a correct worming programme you should have little trouble.

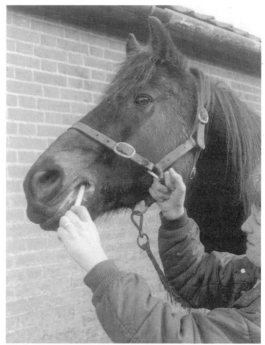

Fig. 37 Worming your mare just prior to foaling will help to reduce the number of transmittable worm larvae passed to the foal through the milk.

Worm control

Some treatments are more effective at certain times of the year so ensure you are using an appropriate one. In general:

• When dosed at regular six-to eight-weekly intervals, a broad-spectrum wormer will control large and small redworms, as well as seatworms and pinworms.

• Dose with an appropriate wormer for bots in late autumn.

• Double-dose with an appropriate wormer in late autumn and the following mid-summer to kill tapeworms.

• Worming your mare just prior to foaling will reduce the number of transmittable worm larvae passed to the foal through her milk.

Inoculation against equine influenza and tetanus (universally referred to as 'flu and tet') should also be considered. Provided your mare has received the initial course for both flu and tet, and yearly boosters thereafter, she will pass some immunity on to the foal through her colostrum. However, if the booster falls more than four months prior to foaling, it may be beneficial to give the mare an extra booster. The optimum time for doing this is two to four weeks prior to foaling, which will offer the foal maximum protection just after birth – its most vulnerable time.

WEIGHT GAIN

Putting on weight is the most obvious change in pregnant mares. Monitoring your mare's weight from the outset is a good idea, as you can then judge whether she is putting on weight as desired. To be accurate you need to assess your mare's weight before she is put in foal. The most accurate way of determining this is by putting your mare on a weighbridge. These are located at various points around the country and your local highways department should be able to tell you where they are in your area. A couple of the main feed manufacturers have portable weighbridges, which they take to various events and large yards. If they are coming near to where you live you might be able to persuade them to weigh your mare for you.

Alternatively you will have to use a weigh-tape. To assess your mare's weight in this way you will need to take a measurement of her 'heart girth', which is taken around her abdomen just behind the withers, and of her length from the point of shoulder to the point of buttocks. These two measurements should then be put in to the following equation to determine her overall bodyweight:

Bodyweight (kg) = heart girth (cm)^2 x length (cm) ÷ 8717 = overall bodyweight in kilograms.
Bodyweight (lb) = heart girth (inches)^2 x length (inches) ÷ 241.3 = overall bodyweight in pounds.

Once you know your mare's pre-pregnancy bodyweight you can check her weight weekly. For the first six months or so she will not put on very much weight, so you are simply checking to ensure she is not losing weight. However, during the last three or four months she can put on as much as a third of her pre-pregnancy bodyweight.

Fig. 38 Provided that all safety precautions are taken it is often beneficial to ride the in-foal mare for some months prior to foaling, as this will help to keep the muscles toned up, which can help with the birth.

EXERCISE

Having a foal is not tantamount to retirement for your mare: you should at all times be thinking of keeping her 'fit to foal'.

A question that many owners ask is, can I still ride my mare? In my opinion it is perfectly safe, and even beneficial to do so, *provided* you are sensible and even more safety-conscious than you have ever been. Keeping a mare in work helps to keep her muscles toned up. This will help her to carry the foal more comfortably and will give her more strength when it comes to expelling the foal at birth. Exercise will also help to prevent water retention (oedema), which can be evident in the legs and underbelly. However, jumping,

galloping, or kicking pregnant mares in the abdomen if they are sluggish, is not advisable. It is unnecessarily stressful to her, and in any case increases the risk of miscarriage, which is foolish. You should also take more care of dangers such as slippery surfaces and pot holes.

Four months prior to foaling, exercise should be confined to slow paces, only walking when your mare nears three months to go. If your mare is due to foal in April it is sensible to stop riding her altogether late in January or early February. Each mare takes to pregnancy differently so be guided by her attitude, general health and mobility. Some mares become uncooperative when ridden, which is obviously their way of telling you that they are not comfortable and would rather be

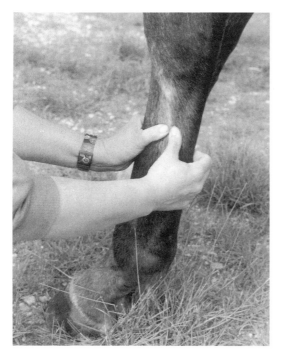

Fig. 39 A brisk massage twice daily to the lower limbs can help to reduce the risk of oedema.

temporarily retired to the 'maternity paddock'. Others will stand at the gate waiting for you to come and exercise them.

When you do eventually cease riding it is still a good idea to lead your mare out in-hand. While she may get enough exercise out in the paddock, leading her about will help prevent her from becoming bored. If your mare does suffer from oedema in the limbs once riding ceases, you can give them a brisk massage twice daily. Do this in the direction of the heart as this encourages venous return.

THE FOAL'S DEVELOPMENT

Usually, the only concern of 'expecting' foal owners is that their mare carries the foal to term without complication and that she delivers a normal, healthy foal that thrives. However, while you are waiting for the event to happen, you may be curious as to what is happening inside your mare.

The organ that allows nourishment of the foal and disposal of its waste matter is called the placenta, which also acts as a natural barrier against undesirable outside influences. The placenta is attached to the wall of the uterus, and is attached to the foetus by the umbilical cord. The umbilical cord acts as the channel through which blood flows to and from the foetus. The foetus itself is surrounded by amniotic fluid, which is encased inside a membrane called the amnion. Between the amnion and the placenta is another fluid called allantoic fluid. Together, the amnion and placental membrane forms the afterbirth. The developing foal is therefore very secure within the mare's body and is cushioned against external forces.

Although the foetus takes 50 per cent of its genetic make-up from its dam (*see* Chapter 2), it is a separate entity with tissues and blood composition that are foreign to its mother. Although it is not obvious to the onlooker, the foetus increases in size at a terrific rate. From the size of a grain of rice at fertilization it will have increased in size to about 10cm (2in) in two to three weeks. Within the first three weeks, blood vessels will be developing and by four weeks it will be forming into the shape of a foal, with limb 'buds' and internal organs. As you might expects the first things to develop are those for general survival – organs such as the heart and liver – whereas the foal's coat will not develop until after the tenth month of pregnancy, as this is

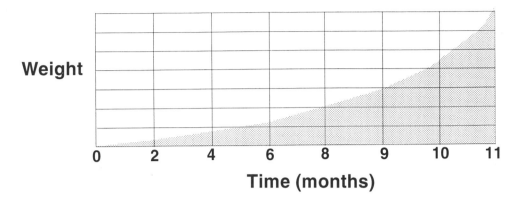

Fig. 40 Weight gain of foetus.

only necessary for the foal's survival after birth.

A foal born after 320 days of pregnancy is considered to be normal; one born before this is said to be premature. It is thought that the foetus signals to the mare when it is mature enough to be delivered, but that the mare is able to withhold delivering it until she feels the time is right. This may be to enable mares in the wild to deliver their foal during the hours of darkness when there is less danger from predators: by morning the foal would be up on its feet and strong enough to run with the herd.

THE FOALING BOX

Even if a mare lives out all year round, it is still safest to bring her into a stable for her to deliver her foal. This way she can be quietly observed and any assistance needed can be offered immediately. The minimum size for a foaling box for a horse is 4.5 x 6m (15 x 20ft), but ideally it should be 4.8 x 7.5m (16 x 24ft). If you have never seen a mare foal before you will be quite surprised to see the amount of pacing up

and down that she does in a short space of time, and she will use all of the available space in order to choose her spot for delivery.

The box should be thoroughly disinfected, and a deep, clean, dry bed of straw laid down. Some people put down a layer of wood chipping under the straw, but it is my experience that the mare digs it all up anyway, and the woodchips then get stuck on to the newly born foal, which is undesirable.

The mare should be brought into the box from six weeks before her due date to allow her to become accustomed to the environment and to give the box 'her smell.' This will provide enough time for the straw to 'bed down' underneath, although the bed must be kept extremely clean and plenty deep enough. You should treat every day as though it could be the day she delivers; then you cannot be caught out. The last thing your mare needs is you rushing in to put more straw down just before she delivers.

From a safety point of view the foaling box should have all projections such as mangers and salt-lick holders removed.

While you may feel a salt-lick holder is far too highly placed for it to be any danger to a foal, mares do get up and down when delivering, and so the foal's legs or head could get damaged before it is even fully delivered. It has also been known for a mare to drop her foal into a manger. Imagine what might happen if you were not on hand immediately to help the foal on to the floor.

Lastly you should ensure that the box has a top door that will close securely, and that there are no draughts.

Foaling away from home

If you do not have a suitable foaling box, or are unable to attend the mare yourself, by far the safest course of action is to send your mare to a stud willing to foal her down for you. Obviously this will incur keep and foaling charges, but it is a far better option than simply leaving your mare to get on with it in an unsuitable environment. While most mares do foal without any complications it is simply not worth taking the risk. However, if you can foal your mare at home (and with the advent of foaling alarms and cameras – *see* pages 65–67 – this has become easier) you will be enriched by the experience. Watching a foal being born is a truly wonderful experience, whether you have never seen it, or have witnessed it a hundred times before.

ABORTION OR PREMATURE FOALING

As we said at the beginning of the chapter the average mare carries her foal for around 340 days. Abortion is said to occur when a foal is carried for less than 300 days. Abortion can be said to be 'early' or 'late': early abortions are those happening within the first three months of pregnancy; late abortions are those that occur thereafter. The difference between the two is that an early abortion usually results in 'absorption' of the embryo: rather than being expelled from the mare's body, the foetus and its membranes are absorbed, so there is no outward trace of the event. Late abortions happen between the third and eighth month, where evidence of the foetus having been expelled may be seen in the stable or paddock. A foal born after 300 days is best described as premature. Foals born after the 300-day period have a chance of life and the further they get to towards a full-term pregnancy the better their chances. Such foals will require a great deal of care, but anyone wishing to breed their own foal should be prepared for such an eventuality.

If your mare aborts, the most important thing is to find out why it happened, as this may determine future plans for your mare. The first thing to establish is whether the cause was infection related. Infections can be quite damaging as an affected mare may abort in a short space of time. Infections may be caused by bacteria or fungus, from microbes that attack the placenta and/or the organs of the foetus. But the most serious of infectious abortions is caused by a virus called Equine Herpes Virus, known as EHV 1. In fact, this virus attacks the respiratory tract, and abortion happens almost as an accidental symptom. The first signs are a nasal discharge and sometimes a mild fever, but the affected horse may not appear to be too unwell and in a substantial amount of cases no symptoms are seen. Abortion may then (but not necessarily) follow. Most commonly, abortion caused by EHV 1 occurs between the seventh and nine months of pregnancy. Mares thought to have aborted as a result of EHV 1 should be isolated, and those who care for them should not care for other mares without first disinfecting themselves and their clothing. A specialist veterinary surgeon may then be called to examine the dead foetus and perhaps take a biopsy of the mare's uterus in order to diagnose the cause of the abortion.

Of the non-infectious causes of abortion, twins are the most common; and this will occur between the sixth and ninth month of pregnancy. A small number of twin pregnancies may be carried to full term but the resulting foals may be very weak, or one or both may be born dead, or die soon after birth. Twin pregnancies have on occasion managed to produce two live foals that have both lived, but these are very rare. It has been established that about 80 per cent of twin pregnancies abort, and of the 20 per cent that do carry to full term one or both of the foals usually die. Horses are fairly unusual in their inability to bear twins. In simple terms, the problem faced by twins is the lack of uterine space and competition for placental nourishment. At best each twin will have an equal, but reduced, space in which to develop. However, it frequently happens that the area is unequally shared and one foal occupies a greater amount of space than the other, or even sections off the other foal into the tip of one of the uterine horns. In the majority of these cases one of the twins dies, which causes the abortion of both foetuses.

Other causes of abortion include damage to the placenta, a problem with the umbilical cord causing the foetus to be starved of oxygen, drugs inadvisably given to the mare, and serious illness in the mare. However, it has to be said that most mares carry healthy foals to full term, so while abortion can be very distressing, it is still quite unlikely that it will happen to your mare. All you can do is to take all sensible precautions against your mare becoming upset; in particular these include avoiding:

• Sudden changes of environment.
• Sudden changes of diet.
• Transportation of a mare who is known to fret.
• Shock.

Diagnosing the Twin Pregnancy

The advent of ultrasound scanning, means that twin pregnancies can now be detected at a very early stage. This allows for intervention by the veterinary surgeon. If the mare has become pregnant early into the stud year, she may be left for some days to see if one of the foetuses fails to survive and is then resorbed. She will then be rescanned and if only one foetus shows up, nature is said to have taken its course. If both foetuses are still evident, the veterinary surgeon may try to 'pinch' one, that is physically try to extract one, so that the pregnancy may progress with one foetus as normal. If this fails, which may be the case if both are very close together, then the pregnancy may be terminated and the mare covered again.

• Exposure to adverse weather conditions.

Abortion can have after-effects although these are unlikely to affect your mare's chances of breeding again, unless she has an underlying condition that prevents her from doing so. If the abortion causes damage to the uterus it may affect your mare's fertility. Other problems include metritis (inflammation of the uterus) and laminitis.

6 Preparing for the Birth

An easy way to work out the likely foaling date is to count eleven months and five days from the last service by the stallion, or by artificial insemination. For example, a mare covered on 1 May one year will have an expected foaling date of around 5 April the following year. However, although you will have this 'expected' date, a delivery of two weeks before or after this date is still quite normal. You should be prepared to put your mare under close observation four weeks prior to her 'expected' date. Some mares have been known to go as late as four weeks, so do not be alarmed if this happens to your mare. If your mare should give you any cause for concern as her time draws near or passes, talk to your veterinary surgeon who will be able to put your mind at rest. One of the things about a normal foaling is that there is such a variation in times and signs that to the inexperienced it may appear anything but 'normal'.

OBSERVATIONS

As the expected date for the foal's arrival draws near, the mare's body undergoes many changes. However, some mares will show quite a few signs that the birth is getting near, others will show none, which is extremely unhelpful to anyone foaling down a mare for the first time. One of the most important things to bear in mind is that mares prefer to foal when they feel least threatened. If you are constantly peering over the door, or rushing in and out of the box every time she moves, you are likely to cause her a great deal of stress. If you are unable to watch her from a remote place by using a closed-circuit television, the next best thing is to have a little peep-hole in her stable where you can keep a watchful eye on her movements without unduly disturbing her.

During the weeks leading up to foaling you may observe a difference in your mare. As every mare is an individual it is impossible to lay down any hard and fast rules. However, what follows is a description of the pattern of most foalings. Your mare may conform to this pattern or she may show none of the signs or behaviour described. The only way to ensure you are present at the birth is to ensure your mare is watched (unobserved by her) for twenty-four hours a day.

Many mares become slightly less energetic and may simply stand about in the paddock as if 'waiting for something to happen'. Often a relaxing of the muscles around the quarters is seen and the mare may go off her food. Loss of appetite is

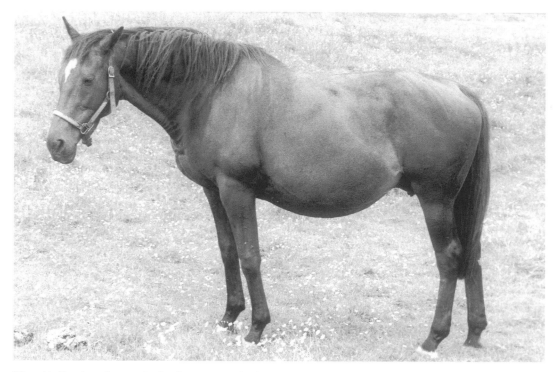

Fig. 41 During the weeks leading up to the birth your mare may stand about a lot as if 'waiting for something to happen'.

Fig. 42 Shortly before foaling, some mares show extremely unusual behaviour, even turning nasty towards other horses or their owners.

caused by the foal taking up so much room that it presses on the stomach, so that when the mare eats she finds she has little space for the food consumed and becomes very uncomfortable. In order to ensure your mare still gets sufficient nutrition you may have to split her normal feeds into lots of smaller ones.

Some mares show extremely unusual behaviour. Individuals have been known to dig great big holes in the paddock, bite at their sides and turn really nasty towards other horses, or even humans. However, such behaviour does not last and is merely an indication of the way the mare is feeling.

The birth may be imminent when one or more of the following signs are present, although some mares show these signs for days before the birth:

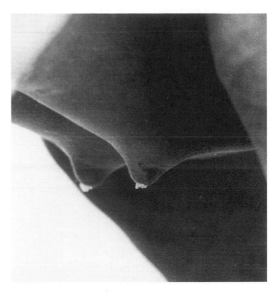

Fig. 43 'Waxing up' is a sure sign that something is about to happen fairly soon.

• A filling and hardening of the udders (known as bagging up), which take on a shiny appearance. The udders will start to fill as much as six weeks prior to the birth and will appear more swollen in the mornings if the mare has been stabled the night before. During exercise in the field the udder tends to reduce in size. However, it is not until a few days before foaling, or even on the day of foaling, that the udder fully 'bags up'.
• 'Waxing up': an off-white sticky substance (the first milk, known as colostrum) forms as a 'cork' on the ends on the nipples. While your mare may have had her nipples plugged with a crystallized substance which is hardly visible to the eye for some months before foaling, 'waxing up' is quite different as it is clearly visible. Waxing up usually occurs between forty-eight and four hours prior to the birth.
• Running milk: milk can be seen down

the mare's hind legs, and may be seen to drip or even pour out of the nipples. This event can be spasmodic, with more wax forming inbetween times. (If your mare is heavily running milk it is a good idea to collect and freeze all that you can in order to give it to the foal soon after birth to ensure that the foal receives enough colostrum.)
• Softening of the muscles of the hindquarters, giving the mare a 'poor' look.
• Softening of the vulva, which becomes distended, moist and sometimes puffy. You should be aware of your mare's normal vulva conformation as there can be a marked difference between horses, especially between maidens and those who have foaled before.
• Filled legs.
• General unease: perhaps pacing around the field or box, and pawing at the ground.

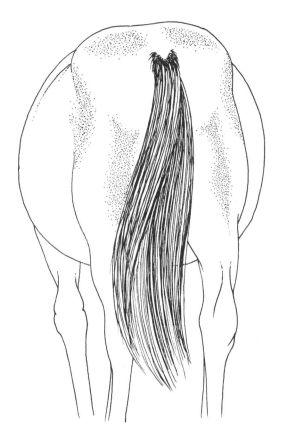

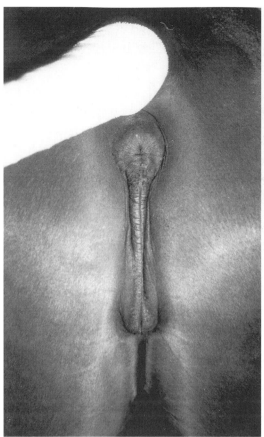

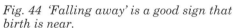

Fig. 44 'Falling away' is a good sign that birth is near.

Fig. 45 The vulva often becomes distended just prior to birth.

By now you will most certainly be ready for the birth. (When I foaled a mare for the first time I sat up for two weeks 'waiting' before she finally delivered.) Do not believe anyone who says you will just 'know' when the foal is coming – you certainly will not, especially if you have never foaled a mare before! Additionally, do not listen to people who tell you that heavily pregnant mares never lie down. Many certainly do. (Some of my mares lie flat out and grunt and groan, but they are simply fast asleep!) However, with all the

best intentions in the world you really are never prepared for the sight of the actual event. You will probably find it all quite magical if it is the first time you have witnessed it, although some people do become distressed at seeing their mares going through birth.

When your mare starts to get hot, paces around, digs up the bed, tries to stale without too much success, and generally behaves as though she has a bout of colic, you can rest assured that you will have your foal within a hour or two. If you are really unlucky, your mare will simply lie down and deliver her foal without preamble; but then that is not a problem because you will be ready for it – right? One last thing, given half a chance your mare will produce her foal during the half an hour that you go indoors for a cup of tea. The best advice: take a flask out with you!

EQUIPMENT

When foaling a mare, you must be prepared for all eventualities. First of all you will need a large disinfected container – perhaps a plastic bucket with a lid or a large polythene container with a lid. Inside this you should put:

1. A can of antiseptic spray.
2. Two pairs of surgical gloves (available from chemists or veterinary surgeries).
3. A large clean towel or sheet.
4. Sterilized scissors in an airtight polythene bag.
5. A clean plastic jug (500ml = 1 pint is ideal).
6. A baby's feeding bottle and two lamb's teats, both sterilized and placed in an airtight bag.
7. A jar of petroleum jelly.
8. A bottle of liquid paraffin.
9. A syringe (ideally an enema syringe).
10. An old, large jumper or a foal rug.
11. Another clean bucket, in which you should place a bar of soap, a bottle of antiseptic liquid and a towel for washing your hands before assisting the birth is necessary.
12. A good book to read while you are waiting . . .

For a normal foaling you are only likely to require items one, two and three (and eleven and twelve); however, you should prepare the rest of the items so that they are to hand if you need them.

Closed circuit television (CCTV)

Opinions differ greatly on the subject of 'foaling on television'. Those who have stayed up all night to observe a foaling mare are against it mainly because they feel you should be on hand immediately, and in some ways they feel it is cheating. I simply cannot agree with this view. Foaling on television has revolutionized foaling for the small breeder, who may also have a family to see to and other commitments that keep them inside the house at night-time. However, I do agree that foaling monitors should only be used to observe the mare before foaling in order not to miss the event. Once the mare is observed on screen as foaling imminently, you should go down to the stable in order to assist if necessary. In any event, there is nothing like seeing your own foal being born before your eyes. One of the dangers with 'foaling on television' is that you are quite likely to fall asleep since watching a mare who is not in labour is extremely boring. It may be fine on the first night; you get an insight into how she occupies the hours of darkness, but after the fourth, fifth, or even fourteenth, it does become a little monotonous. In order to counteract this, you will need to set an hourly alarm clock once the mare shows signs that the foaling is near.

Another factor to consider is the cost, and whether this outweighs the inconvenience of sitting up in the stables. A CCTV system can cost as much as a good leather saddle, and you may use it for only two weeks of the year. Only you can decide whether the cost is worth it to you, although if the cost of purchase is the only prohibitive factor you can hire systems for two or three weeks at a time for a relatively small sum of money.

All CCTV systems require some lighting in order to provide acceptable pictures. In general the better the lighting the better the picture, although you have to balance this against the upset this might cause to the mare. (This is another reason that some people disapprove of CCTV.) A compromise is the best bet, opting for the dullest lighting that will allow you to see what your mare is doing. Generally a single 40 watt or perhaps 60 watt light bulb correctly positioned will be adequate for a 4.8 x 7.5m (16 x 24ft) foaling box. Try both and then decide which is most suitable.

The type of lens needed is also a consideration. This is governed by the size and shape of the foaling box. Generally a square box requires an ultra-wide lens; a rectangular box a wide lens and a long narrow box a standard lens. You will need to try out different positions for the camera before you can determine the best place to site it.

Most systems are extremely simple and straightforward to install and some can be connected to a video recorder so that you can record the whole event. Some require a mains point within 25 metres (27yd) of the camera position; others run straight from camera to monitor without the need for a separate mains supply. Ensure you choose a model that is pre-wired and ready for installation. All you will then require are suitable screws and a screwdriver to fix the camera bracket to the wall. Most hire systems are despatched in this way, but do check this when ordering.

Foaling alarms

A foaling alarm is designed to sense when a mare is going to foal and then sound the alarm. A sensor and transmitter are fitted to a breastplate which is anchored to the mare by a roller. The sensor detects any significant change in the mare's body temperature and the transmitter then sends a signal which activates the alarm on the receiver. It is quite usual for the alarm to be sounded about half an hour before the mare starts to deliver, as this is when she starts to 'hot up'.

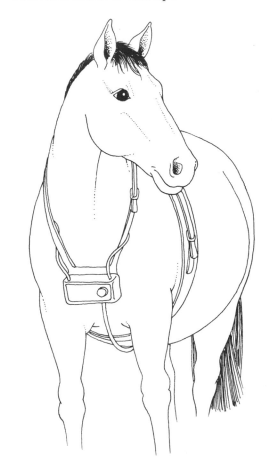

Fig. 46 A foaling alarm correctly fitted.

Obviously, if the mare's temperature rises for some other reason, perhaps colic, then the alarm will still sound. Once the alarm has been raised and you confirm that birth is imminent it is a good idea to remove the alarm for the mare's own comfort when foaling. It is essential that any projecting items are removed from the stable (which should have been done in any case) otherwise the foaling alarm and its harness are in danger of getting caught up. While a foaling alarm does not hurt the mare in any way, it does appear to irritate some mares. If this is the case, you may have to put a bib on your mare to prevent her from trying to rip the harness off. Alarms may be used instead of, or as well as, CCTV, and although they are usually quite reliable, they should not be regarded as a fail-safe system. It is still a good idea to physically look at the mare at regular intervals if you suspect the birth is very near.

Final preparation

Once your mare is obviously about to foal you should put a headcollar and tail bandage on her. The headcollar may be your only hope of catching the mare if she becomes nervous, or extremely protective of her foal. The tail bandage will allow you to see exactly what is happening and will prevent the tail from becoming clogged up with the discharges of foaling. It is a good idea to remove the water bucket from the stable and to put a bale of straw inside the door to keep your mare from lying down too near the door, and to prevent draughts from underneath it penetrating the stable. Once these measures are in place, it is simply a case of waiting, observing, but most of all restraining the impulse to rush into the stable every time your mare moves.

PATIENCE

If you have never foaled a mare before (and even if you have), you are likely to be far more anxious than your mare in the days leading up to the foal's expected arrival. If the foal arrives near to time, your patience will probably be quite strong. However, if your mare is overdue, you may become fractious. You start to imagine that there must be something wrong and that you should be 'doing something'. However, it is at this time that you need to be patient. Ring your veterinary surgeon if you really feel something is not right, but in the majority of cases he will simply tell you to wait. It is very unlikely that your veterinary surgeon will induce your mare (provoke her to deliver her foal) as this carries a high risk of foal mortality.

In order to fill your time while you are waiting you can always clean the tack, disinfect all the stables, sweep the yard, clean the paddock of droppings . . . the list is endless and you will have your foal before you know it.

7 The Birth

Most foalings are quick and uncomplicated. Once the birth is imminent, the foaling process is a fairly predictable one and provided you are well prepared for the event it will be a marvellous, if anxious, experience.

LABOUR

While there are no hard and fast rules for the signs of imminent labour, once your mare is in labour the sequence of events will follow a clearly predictable path. The act of delivering a foal appears to take a short time from start to finish, but the mare may have been in labour for some hours before she shows any visible signs of discomfort. Labour is divided into three distinct stages:

1. Stage one: involuntary uterine contractions move the foal into position ready for birth. The cervix will relax and dilate to facilitate passage of the foal.
2. Stage two: the foal enters the mare's pelvis and passes through the cervix aided by the mare's bearing down to deliver the foal to the outside world.
3. Stage three: delivery of the afterbirth.

First stage

Onset of labour until breaking of the waters

At first you may simply observe unease in your mare. This may last for some hours and she may pace around the field or stable showing obvious signs of discomfort. This may be spasmodic as the discomfort is caused by her contractions which come at regular intervals. At first these bouts of discomfort may come some distance apart, but as she nears the second stage of birth the contractions start to come more rapidly and to increase in strength. Other signs that are a good indication that your mare is experiencing the first stage of birth are:

- Swishing of the tail.
- Stamping of the feet.
- Looking around at her sides.
- Biting her sides.
- Rubbing her tail.
- Getting up and down.
- Raising her tail.
- Sweating

Once your mare starts to sweat, her foal will usually arrive within an hour or two. However, occasionally, all these signs are transitory and the mare returns to normal, only to give birth a day or two later. These cases are not common, but when they occur it is thought that the mare shows these signs in response to the foal's moving into position, or in response to 'trial' contractions, similar to 'Bracks and Hicks' contractions in humans.

At the transition between the first and second stage of labour your mare will probably get up and down many times, but at some point she will go down (although be prepared, as a few mares foal standing up!) and the waters (allantoic fluid) will come away. The water may break with a whoosh or perhaps just a slow stream; either way it indicates the end of the first stage and the beginning of the foal's expulsion in to the world. (If your mare is caslicked it is at this point that you should open her – *see* page 83. From now on it should take about twenty minutes for the foal to be born. Note the time that your

mare's waters break. This will help you to judge if all is going to plan, or whether veterinary help may be needed.

Second stage

Breaking of the waters until the expulsion of the foal

Once your mare's waters have broken she will usually lie down and begin to strain. She may grunt, groan and generally make some pretty awful noises, so do not become too distressed at this – it is quite normal. The first thing you will notice is what looks like a bulb of water appearing between the distended lips of the vulva. This is simply the membrane, or 'amnion' as it is correctly known, filled with amni-

Fig. 47 The point of no return: breaking of the waters indicates the end of the first stage.

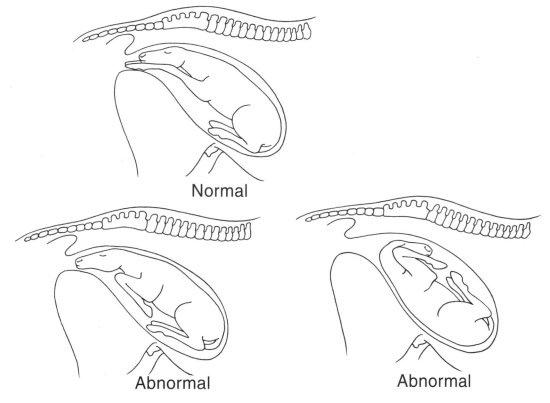

Normal

Abnormal

Abnormal

Fig. 48 Foal presentation at birth

otic fluid which has protected the foal inside the womb. You may also see the tips of the forefeet poking through. Many people will tell you that this is the time you should check to see if the muzzle, and indeed forelegs, are lying in the correct position. This is a good idea, but in all honesty unless you have been at previous foalings with someone experienced showing you what to look for, or more correctly what to 'feel' for, then you might find this a little difficult. It does not matter how many pictures of the birth you look at, what to 'feel' for cannot be explained with lucidity: to the inexperi-

enced everything resembles slimy bumps! However, what you should be trying to make out are two forelegs (one will be slightly in front of the other), and the foal's muzzle lying on top of these. If you decide to check that the foal is coming in the correct position, ensure you scrub your hands and arms with soap and water first so as to prevent any infection from entering the mare's body. If for any reason you suspect that the foal is not being presented in this correct position now is the time to call the vet with great haste (*see* Chapter 8).

Next you will actually see the foal's

Fig. 49 A 'bulb' of water appears between the distended lips of the vulva.

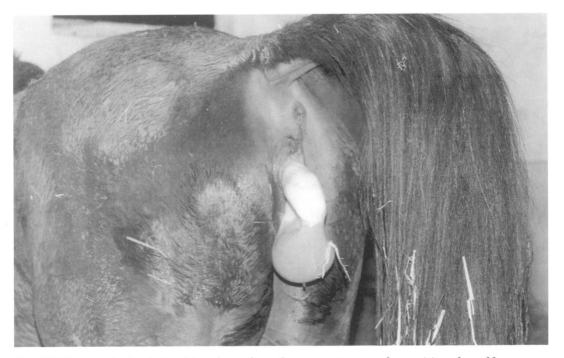

Fig. 50 The tip of a forefoot poking through as the mare gets up and repositions herself.

muzzle, lying on top of the two forelegs, followed by the foal's head lying on top of the forearms. Next to come are the foal's shoulders and your mare may need to make what seems to be a tremendous effort in order to push them out. In fact, she may even get up at this point and pace around before settling herself down again to deliver the forehead and shoulders.

Once the head and shoulders are delivered, the foal is past the point of return and, if they have not already done so naturally, the membranes over the muzzle and face should be broken to allow air into the foal's lungs. However, a word of caution here: in no circumstances should the membranes be broken before the shoulders are delivered, as your mare may get up again allowing the foal to slip back into the delivery passage. Should this

happen without the protection of the membranes around the muzzle the foal is in danger of fluid entering its nose, and therefore lungs, which could lead to complications, if not prove fatal.

Once the shoulders are delivered the rest of the foal will simply slip out. The foal's body will still be partially covered in membranes, and the foal will still be attached to the placenta inside the mare by the umbilical cord. Do not be too quick to interfere at this point. Provided the foal is breathing it is best left to the attention of its mother: do not attempt to break the cord. Contrary to what other people may tell you, the foal will come to no harm if left attached to the placenta, even for some time. When either the mare gets up, or the foal begins to struggle to its feet, the umbilical cord will break naturally in

Fig. 51 Next, the other forefoot appears . . .

Fig. 52 . . . closely followed by the foal's muzzle lying along the top of both forelegs. The membranes are still intact at this point.

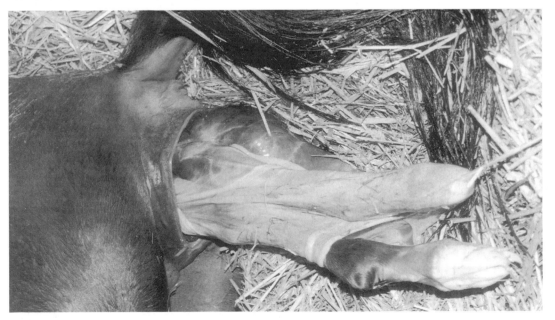

Fig. 53 The foal's head, lying along its forearms, and the tip of the forefoot breaks through the membrane. Note the soft, white feet.

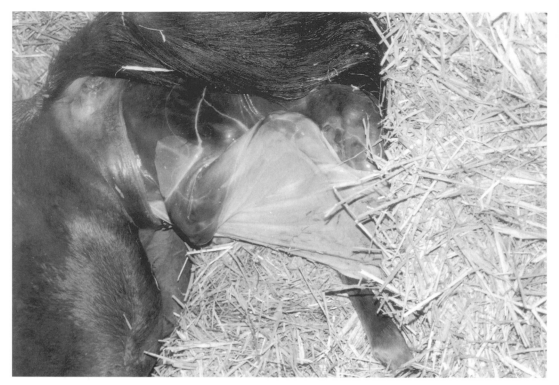

Fig. 54 The most difficult part of the birth for the mare is delivering the shoulders, and your mare may make what seems like a tremendous effort in order to do so.

the correct place. While the foal is still attached to the placenta there are a few things still happening. The 'valve' between mare and foal is closing so preventing the exit of any blood from the foal's body, but it will still be extracting valuable substances from the placenta through the umbilical cord. So you can see that premature severing of the umbilical cord is detrimental, rather than beneficial. (There are a few occasions when you may need to cut the cord but these are abnormal and are dealt with in Chapter 8).

Your mare may remain lying down for a good thirty minutes after the birth.

Giving birth is an extremely draining experience, and during this time she will be recouping her strength. Do not disturb her. If she is whinnying and trying to rise to greet her foal, but without much success, you can gently pull the foal around to the front of her where she can lick and mother it, but you should quickly leave the stable or else your mare may try to rise. Do be careful not to put the foal in the way of her forelegs, otherwise she might damage it when she does eventually get up. At the point when your mare first licks her foal to dry the coat, vital bonding is occurring – **leave them alone**.

Fig. 55 Once the shoulders have been delivered your mare may rest for a while. If the foal has not broken through the membranes you must break the membrane yourself at this point to allow air into the foal's lungs.

Fig. 56 Your mare may rest for some time with the foal's hind legs still inside her. Do not be too quick to interfere, but do check that the foal is breathing.

Fig. 57 At the point when your mare first licks her foal, vital bonding is occurring.

Third stage

Passing of the afterbirth

Once the cord has broken you will see part of the membranes, or the afterbirth, hanging down between your mare's hind legs. Your mare will be experiencing further contractions at this point, which are intended to help her expel the afterbirth. If the membranes are dragging on the floor, you can double them up and tie them together with clean string for your mare's comfort and to prevent tearing. The afterbirth is usually delivered within an hour or two. Sometimes it is delivered in minutes; at other times it can take a good few hours. However, if the afterbirth has not been delivered within eight hours

of foaling you should call your veterinary surgeon, who will give her an injection to cause the afterbirth to separate from the uterine wall, whereupon he will remove it manually and flush the mare out. In no circumstances should you attempt to pull the afterbirth free yourself. It may still be attached to the uterine wall and if you pull on it, you will simply tear it. This will cause some parts of it to remain inside your mare, which can lead to septicaemia.

Until the afterbirth is delivered, your mare may still show signs of pain, perhaps rolling, pawing at the ground or generally displaying colicky symptoms. Again, this is normal. However, if these bouts of pains are prolonged or appear severe, then it is a good idea to have your veterinary

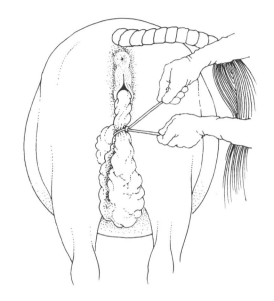

Fig. 58 Tying up the placenta.

When the mare has finished foaling, she will probably appreciate a drink of water, and perhaps something to eat. However, *do not* give her a bran mash (*see* Chapter 9); rather, offer her a little of her usual feed with some sugar beet in it.

surgeon check your mare over in case there are complications.

Once the afterbirth is delivered you should put it into a bucket or black polythene sack, so that it can be inspected for completeness. It cannot be stressed enough that you **must** ensure the afterbirth is complete. In most cases the afterbirth is expelled inside out, that is with the whitish, smooth surface outwards. However, in some cases (although usually this is in abnormal cases) it is delivered with the red, velvety surface facing outwards. However, you need not concern yourself at this stage. Your task now is to ensure that the afterbirth is intact. A complete afterbirth appears as a whole sack, with just one opening through which the foal passed. If there are tears, you should ensure that they will close together like a jigsaw. If not, then it is likely that your mare has retained some of the afterbirth, and there-fore veterinary attention must be sought. In any case keep the afterbirth for inspection by your veterinary surgeon, after which it should be disposed of by burning.

THE HIPPOMANE

When picking up the afterbirth ready for inspection you may find a brown, rubbery, oval object called the Hippomane (also known as the 'milt', 'melt', 'melch', or 'foal bread'). This is about 12cm (5fiin) in length and is expelled with the afterbirth. It is unknown what it is, or what precise purpose it serves, although it is known to contain high concentrations of various salts, including sodium, potassium, calcium, phosphorous and magnesium. When found, it used to be kept outside the foaling box as a lucky charm, to bring the foal good health, although the name 'hippomane' comes from the Greek word meaning 'horse madness'!

Most foalings do proceed closely to these guidelines. However should anything give you cause for concern it is always a sensible precaution to call your vet. If there are complications, speed is of the essence, but should he arrive to be greeted by a lively little foal and a contented mare he will be the first to congratulate you.

Fig. 59 The hippomane.

VETERINARY EXAMINATION

Even when a foaling has gone 'according to the book', it is a good idea to let your vet know that your foal is born, and ask him to call as a matter of routine during surgery hours. He will then be able to inspect the foal, and may possibly pick up small things that you may not have noticed yourself. In any event, it is always reassuring to have a vet give both your mare and foal a clean bill of health. He will examine the foal for defects such as contracted tendons, limb deformities, parrot mouth, hare lip, and other malformations. He will also check the foal's vital signs and will probably give the foal routine injections against tetanus and joint ill.

8 Complications and Veterinary Care

In any case other than a normal foaling, veterinary attention must be sought immediately.

A mare in trouble requires skilled help and there is little you can do but try to keep her calm until the vet arrives. However, if you have never foaled down a mare before it can sometimes be difficult to judge whether she is experiencing complications or not, and the unknown can be extremely frightening. Foaling is a completely natural event, but at times it can seem very dramatic. However, to put things in context, you should always remember that the majority of mares have no difficulty in delivering their foals, and most could not care less whether you are present or not. Rather than go through all the things that could go wrong but probably will not, what follows is a guide to the questions most commonly asked by people foaling mares for the first time, together with advice on the correct course of action to take. However, if you always bear in mind the sentence that opened this chapter you will not go far wrong. It always amazes me that so many people spend hundreds of pounds getting their

mare into foal, only to hold off from calling the vet in times of trouble for fear of a large veterinary bill.

My mare went down and her waters broke, but nothing has happened for some time although she is straining vigorously. What should I do?

How long is some time? A couple of minutes or twenty minutes? You should have noted what time your mare's waters broke (see pages 68–69) as once you begin to doubt all is going to plan, minutes can seem like hours. If it is less than five minutes since the waters broke wait a little while longer. At six minutes, you can either examine the mare yourself if you know how to distinguish the correct position of the two forefeet and the muzzle (*see* pages 70–76), or you can call the veterinary surgeon. If you can feel the feet and muzzle wait to see if they appear in the next two to four minutes. At ten minutes you *must* call the vet for assistance if nothing has appeared from the vaginal lips. Do not panic. Malposture of the head and forelimbs does not put the foal's life immediately at risk because the umbilical

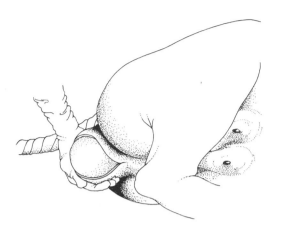

Fig. 60 Normal appearence of foetal membranes.

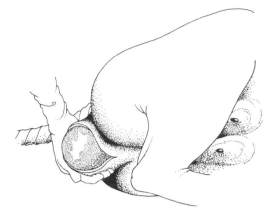

Fig. 61 Unruptured placental membrane.

cord is under no pressure and the membranes are still intact. When the vet arrives he will assess the foal's position and should be able to take correct action to reposition the foal. While awaiting the arrival of the vet, a plentiful supply of hot water, soap, a suitable disinfectant and a towel should be made ready so that there is no delay when he arrives.

My mare is on the floor and straining, but all I can see is a big red balloon, with what looks like a scar on it. I'm pretty sure her waters have not broken. What should I do?

This is probably the placental membrane which has failed to rupture normally. Provided you can see the scar (which distinguishes the placental membrane from a prolapse of the uterus or bladder) you should break the membrane, otherwise stage two of the birth cannot commence. It will probably be quite tough (one of the reasons it did not break of its own accord) so you may need carefully to use a pair of scissors. It is very important

to be sure that you are looking at the placental membrane and not the sac in which the foal is encased. If in any doubt that this is not the placental membrane call the vet immediately and try to keep your mare calm.

I am sure that the foal is coming back to front in the posterior position. What should I do?

Firstly, call your veterinary surgeon. Speed is of the essence here because, while a breech presentation does not delay the delivery, the cord can become compressed and so shut off the foal's oxygen supply. If the vet has not arrived by the time the hocks are out you will have to assist your mare: at each contraction from the mare, pull down on the hind fetlocks so that delivery is as quick as possible. *Do not* pull the foal inbetween contractions. At the end of each contraction you must stop pulling and wait for the next. As soon as the foal is free you must clear the membranes and any mucous from the nose to avoid asphyxiation.

I can see the two forefeet and the head lying along the forearms, but despite my mare's exhaustive straining the delivery is not progressing. Should I assist by pulling the foal?

Yes, providing you are *certain* the presentation is correct (*see* page 70). Wrap a dry sheet or towel around the foal's legs *above* the fetlock joints and, as your mare strains with the next contractions, steadily pull. *Do not* pull when your mare is not straining herself and never pull on the fetlock joints themselves. You may be surprised at the effort needed to pull the foal's shoulders through the birth canal. Once the head and shoulders are through, leave your mare to take a rest.

If despite your efforts the foal is still making no progress, call the vet with haste in case the hind feet have become lodged on the brim of the pelvis. Any major manipulation of the foal's position must only be done by a veterinary surgeon. While waiting for him to arrive, keep your mare standing or walk her around the foaling box.

My mare has delivered the foal's head and shoulders, but the hindquarters are still inside her. Should I pull these free?

No. After the exhaustive efforts of delivering the head and shoulders your mare will naturally take a breather. Leave her in peace. If there is still no progress after five minutes or so, call the vet, as it may be that the foal's pelvis is jammed in the mare's.

The foal is born but the umbilical cord has not broken. Should I cut it?

No. If you look at the cord directly after birth you will see that it is still red, and if you feel it you will detect a pulse running through it. This is because the foal is still receiving oxygen from its dam's blood. As this diminishes the cord turns white and more brittle, and when the foal struggles to its feet or your mare rises it will naturally break.

My mare delivered the afterbirth within half an hour, and the foal is still attached to it by the umbilical cord, which has turned white. Should I cut it?

If the cord does not break naturally you can do so, but do be sure that you are not being hasty. If you bend it in half about 5–7cm (2–3in) from the foal's belly you may find that it is enough to snap it. In some cases the cord is very tough and will need cutting with sterilized scissors; once again, this should be done at the point at which it would normally break naturally – about 5–7cm (2–3in) from the belly. First tie a piece of sterilized cord tightly around the umbilical cord about 3cm (1fiin) from the foal's belly; then tie another piece of cord about 2cm (1in) further away from this. Then, with a pair of sterilized scissors, cut the cord between the two tourniquets. The cut end of the umbilical cord should then be treated with an antiseptic spray.

Having said all this, it cannot be stressed enough that your intervention in severing the cord is an extremely rare necessity. In almost every case it is preferable to leave the matter to nature since surgical severance vastly increases the likelihood of infection in the abdomen.

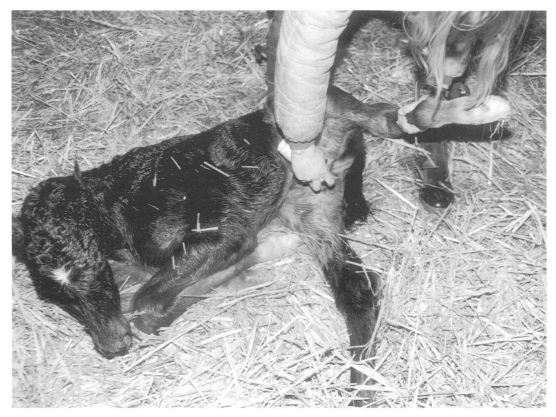

Fig. 62 As soon as the cord snaps the stump should be treated with an antibiotic spray to prevent infection entering the body.

The cord has just snapped. Is there anything I should do?

Yes. Once the cord has snapped you should treat the stump at the foal's belly with antiseptic spray to prevent infection from entering the body.

The cord has snapped, but it is bleeding. What should I do?

Nip the ends together between forefinger and thumb and apply pressure for a few minutes. Treat with antiseptic spray as soon as the bleeding has stopped.

The foal has been born but it appears very weak and is having difficulty breathing. Is there anything I can do to help it?

Yes. First call the vet. While you are waiting for the vet to arrive, use some clean, dry towels to massage the foal vigorously. Gently pump the forelegs backwards and forwards as this will encourage air to be taken in and expelled out of the lungs. The foal can also be shaken head downwards to clear any fluid remaining in the passages. If the foal has stopped breathing altogether you can offer

82

mouth-to-nostril respiration. Close the nostril nearest to the floor with your hand, and make a cup on the upper nostril with your other hand; blow into it so that air goes through your hand into the nostril. Keep the foal warm until the vet arrives.

The foal is making gurgling noises. Is it ill?

Probably not. Many foals make strange noises soon after birth and usually this is no cause for alarm. They are simply trying to rid themselves of fluid and mucous that has collected at the back of the throat. Gently lifting the quarters off the floor will help. If the symptoms persist, or the foal seems otherwise unwell, call the vet.

My mare shows no inclination to lick her foal. What should I do?

Firstly rub the foal briskly with a clean, dry towel to stimulate its circulation. Place the foal on a clean part of the bed and rub some salt on it, as this will encourage the mare to start licking it. If she still refuses your first duty is to the foal, so you will have to persevere until it is dry or, at least, until it starts to thrash about in order to try to get to its feet.

FIRST-AID FOR THE MARE

Most mares require little if any treatment after foaling. If a tail bandage was fitted before the birth this should be removed, and her genital area can be cleansed with warm, soapy water to remove stains, dried fluid and mucous. It is always a good idea to have your vet visit during normal surgery hours to check over both mare and foal. Any tearing of the mare's vulva or vaginal passage should be stitched and the sooner this is attended to after foaling the less painful it will be for the mare and the quicker it will heal. This aspect of care should not be ignored, as failure to repair a tear may result in infection which in turn may prevent the mare from getting in foal again.

Severe bruising of the vagina, perhaps coupled with haematoma and/or blistering of the membrane's lining, will cause the vulva lips to swell and become a deep red-purple in colour. The vet must attend to this with antibiotics and anti-inflammatory drugs, otherwise the mare may become severely infected and have difficulty in urinating.

CASLICK OPERATION

If your mare had difficulty in getting in foal the previous year, it may have been caused by poor perineal conformation (commonly a tilted vulva and sunken anus). This leaves your mare susceptible to infection through a process known as 'windsucking' (not to be confused with the vice of the same name), in which air (and thus bacteria) is drawn into the vagina. Windsucking can prevent a mare from conceiving or from 'holding' once she has conceived. To remedy the condition, your veterinary surgeon may advise that your mare be caslicked. This procedure should not be performed without your consent, as your mare's vulva will require opening immediately prior to foaling (by cutting with a pair of sharp scissors) and re-stitching again afterwards.

The two sides of the upper part of the vulva are trimmed under anaesthetic, and then stitched together again to form a tight seal. Depending on the extent of the

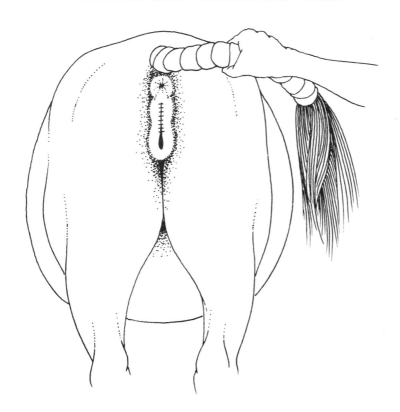

*Fig. 63 A caslicked
mare.*

caslick, some mares may not require opening prior to service by the stallion, but all caslicked mares will require opening during foaling or else they will tear.

You can distinguish a caslicked mare by inserting a surgically gloved finger behind the lips of the vulva and touching the roof of the vagina. If, when you try to pull your finger out without lowering it, you meet resistance, your mare has been caslicked.

On large studs, where veterinary surgeons are on call all the time, caslicked mares do not pose a problem. However, for the individual mare owner, a caslicked mare can cause concern. It can be a worrying experience to open a mare just prior to foaling especially if you are squeamish.

Opening a mare is best done just as the

waters are about to break or when they have just broken. Great care is needed and most veterinary surgeons are of the opinion that the mare's vulva has little feeling at this time, so the cut can be performed without causing pain. That said, it is still a difficult thing to do the first time you have to do it. However, you must be positive and not hesitant. The safest method is to place your index and middle fingers inside the vulva on either side of the caslick and then with one or two positive strokes, cut up the line of the caslick until it is open. Most mares will allow you to do this once they are on the floor. If you have never performed this operation before, it is sensible to seek help or supervision from a more experienced person.

POST-FOALING COMPLICATIONS

Prolapse of the womb

A prolapse of the womb can be caused by the mare overstraining during a difficult birth. It is indicated by a huge, pear-shaped organ appearing between the hind legs, from out of the vagina. It can be a very frightening thing to witness as the structure can hang as low as the hocks. You should call the vet immediately, but keep calm. Although it is an alarming condition the vet will immediately take corrective measures. While awaiting the vet take the weight of the structure by holding it in a clean, warm, moist towel or sheet, as near to the vagina as possible. On arrival the vet will replace the structure within your mare's body and may possibly stitch her to prevent recurrence.

Inflammation of the womb

This condition becomes apparent at between two and ten days after foaling, usually as a result of retained afterbirth when the womb has not contracted properly. However, there are other causes, such as overstraining of the uterus caused by a large foal, intra-uterine haemorrhage, excess retention of blood, or infection.

If an infection is allowed to take hold the mare will quickly go off her appetite and her movements will become stilted. Her coat will become 'staring', and she will have a thick, dark, foul-smelling discharge. Her pulse rates and temperature will increase and pressure over the loin area will be painful. This condition must be treated quickly and professionally, otherwise it may prove fatal.

Mastitis

Otherwise known as inflammation of the udder, this condition can appear at any time during lactation, or soon after weaning. There are various causes, but the symptoms are clear. The udder swells and feels hard and warm. The udder will be extremely painful and if any milk can be drawn off it will be found to be clotted and possibly tinged with blood. Mastitis needs immediate veterinary attention, and it may be possible to remedy the situation so that the mare can continue to suckle her foal. During the painful stage, the foal must be prevented from sucking at the udder and an alternative milk supply if appropriate must be offered.

The foal-proud mare

Some mares are so protective of their new foals that they will not allow you anywhere near it, sometimes to the point of savaging you if you try. This is why it helps to put a headcollar on your mare before foaling (*see* Chapter 6, Final preparation.) Some mares are simply nervous, especially maidens, and a lot of reassurance from you that there is nothing to fear will go a long way towards calming her down. If you know that your mare becomes foal proud, you should attend to the foal as soon after birth as possible, as at this time such mares are usually a little dazed and will tolerate your presence. Leave it until a few hours later and there is no way you will get near their foal! With foal-proud mares the protective period does tend to wear off as time goes by and so you will probably be able to handle the foal within a few weeks. However, the foal-proud mare may present a problem if the foal

Fig. 64 Where's my mum? Some mares seem not to care that much about their foals; others are so protective that you cannot get near the foal.

needs attention for one reason or another. At such times you will simply have to be strict with the mare to the point of muzzling her or even twitching her if she becomes really nasty when you handle the foal.

Refusal to suckle

At the other end of the scale are mares who could not care less about their new foals. They show no inclination to mother the foal and seem only to tolerate them feeding because of the foals' perseverance to do so. You must keep a watchful eye on the foal of such a mare to ensure that it is getting enough food. Some nervous mares can inadvertently prevent their foals from suckling. They may be so overprotective that they refuse to let the foal out of their

sight. Consequently when the foal moves around the back of the mare, towards her udder, she quickly turns around to see where it has gone. Subsequently the foal is deprived of its meal at every attempt and if the situation is not remedied the foal will become weak to the point of exhaustion. Other mares seem to have such a sensitive udder that they squeal and kick every time the foal goes to feed.

In all these cases patience is needed to ensure both mare and foal settle down to a regular feeding pattern. The mare should be held firmly by the headcollar and pushed sideways on to the stable wall so that the only way she can move is by swinging her quarters around to you. The foal will instinctively nuzzle around the dark, shadowy areas of the mare, and once he has successfully fed a few times, the mare should be more relaxed and the

Fig. 65 You must keep a watchful eye that the foal is getting enough food. Obviously this foal is, but she is certainly dragging her dam down. The mare should be fed more in order to compensate for the foal's demands.

foal more confident. If the foal's first bad experiences have made it hesitant you should offer a guiding arm. In some cases you will need to actually clamp the foal's mouth around the teat in order to get it to realize where the food source is. However, such measures are not usually necessary, but if you find yourself in any of these situations you must persevere for as long as it takes to ensure both mare and foal have formed a healthy bond together.

While it should be avoided if at all possible, in some cases a mare may need to be sedated in order to allow her foal to feed. However, this is fairly rare, but still preferable to bottle-feeding the foal.

THE ORPHAN FOAL

Losing a much-loved mare is a heart rending experience and, thankfully, rare. But in the event of the mare's death it is important to remember that there is still a new life that depends upon us for survival. At a time when we are very distressed, we have to pick up the pieces and get on with life in order to ensure that the new foal survives. The first problem is that of there being no colostrum. In some cases it is possible to milk the mare, but often very little can be extracted. However, any amount is better than none. In some cases you may have been able to collect some colostrum before birth (*see* page 63).

87

Fig. 66 *Losing a mare is tragic, but there is still a new life that will depend upon you for survival. This foal is only minutes old, and keeping it alive without its mother will prove a huge commitment.*

As soon as a mare dies there is a major decision to be made: that of keeping the foal or having it put down. The decision to put a foal down may seem abhorrent to many of you, but unless you have 'survived' an orphan foal it is hard to imagine the 24-hour-a-day care that you will need to provide and the constant veterinary attention that it will need to keep it alive. The agonizing decision will be your own, but you should be prepared for a huge commitment in terms of time and expense.

Initially, for the first one or two weeks, the foal will require hourly feeding around the clock. A foal can take in only small amounts at any one time, so it requires

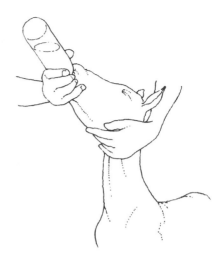

Fig. 67 *Bottle feeding an orphan foal.*

many feeds in order to get sufficient nutrition. At first you will need to use a baby's feeding bottle, then progressing to lambs' and calves' bottles with large teats.

Without a mother the foal requires another source of heat and in such cases a heat lamp is usually the best alternative. A foal will snuggle into the cosy spot and feel that he has a safe place to return to whenever he feels the need for a little comfort.

It is known that the orphan foal can be extremely boisterous, so it must be taught respect every time it is handled. It is important to allow the orphan foal to associate with other horses as soon as possible so that it learns to socialize with them. Otherwise, it will tend to think that you are its family.

If you feel you cannot cope with the demands of an orphan foal, but could not contemplate having it put down, you could try to find a surrogate mare. The National Foaling Bank is known all over the world for providing an adoption service for orphan foals by matching them with a suitable foster mare who has lost her own foal. The service also takes on nearly impossible cases of savaging mares, problem foaling mares (haemolytic, cancer, twinning, etc), and foals that need 24-hour nursing: in a nutshell, any problem that you are unable to cope with yourself. Even if they are unable to find a suitable mare, they can offer you invaluable help and advice. The National Foaling Bank is run by Johanna Vardon and you can contact her at the National Foaling Bank, Meretown Stud, Newport, Shropshire TF10 8BK.

NURSING THE SICK FOAL

Most foals need very little human interference, but those that do require knowledgeable handling in order for the vet to be able to treat them so that they may get better. Caring for a sick foal is a huge responsibility, but things always seem less daunting if you know what to expect and how to handle the foal. It is hoped that the information given in this chapter has prepared you for what to look out for and how to deal with it, but what of the physical side of foal care? How should you handle a sick foal without causing it pain or distress, and what might the veterinary surgeon require when he attends the foal? The vet's job is to diagnose and treat any diseases, but as the foal's owner you have a duty to assist the vet by supporting and handling the foal in order for him to do so. Too many people feel that their duty is over once the vet arrives, but this is just the time when your help is needed most. You may have many duties to perform. For instance if the foal has no suck reflex you will have to

feed it artificially until it does; if it fails to get to its feet after birth you must help it; if it is cold you must keep it warm, and so on. Such duties may only last a matter of hours, but you should be prepared to nurse a sick foal for days or even weeks.

Uneducated handling – even with the best intentions – may cause the foal stress, so do try to learn all you can about foal handling before your mare is due to foal. Struggling is one of the main things you will have to cope with, as any procedure – however small – is distressing to the foal and the only way it knows how to cope is to try to get away from the source of distress. You can help to alleviate much of a foal's stress by placing it in the position that he would normally get himself into, but cannot for some reason. For instance, foals feel vulnerable lying flat on the floor, and in response to distress it will try to manoeuvre itself on to its brisket. If it cannot get on to its brisket it may violently struggle and use up valuable strength in the process. If you can help it onto its brisket you will reduce its stress and so conserve its energy. Similarly you can help a weak foal that is struggling to stand by lifting at the appropriate moment. Once the foal has achieved its aim, it will become calmer. If such measures are taken to calm a weak foal, unnecessary exertion will be avoided and thus the foal will be able to use all its energy to recover from illness.

Common sense should be applied in all situations so that noise and rough handling are avoided and a soothing, calm atmosphere is created. At all costs you should try to get 'in tune' with a sick foal's desires. This may sound ridiculous, but unless you can distinguish between a hungry foal that is simply too weak to feed on its own, and a weak but nevertheless

Fig. 68 A foal that feels vulnerable will try to manoeuvre itself on to its brisket.

Fig. 69 Specially made foal rugs can prove invaluable for early or sick foals.

full foal who simply does not want any further feed at the present time, you may be doing more harm than good in your perseverance to make it feed.

Keeping a Foal Warm

There are various ways of keeping a sick foal warm, but check with the veterinary surgeon that this is what is required before doing so. (A foal with a fever does not need to increase its temperature, for instance.) If warmth is requested and the foal is on its feet you can use a specially made foal rug; if that is not available you can improvise with an old, large jumper to keep it warm. Put the foal's forelegs through the arms of the jumper and pull it back along the loins, but be sure that it does not interfere with the sheath of a colt. The jumper should be snug enough that it will not fly over the foal's head should it jump or roll about. Infra-red lights can be used with good effect, but usually these are not in place in the case of one-time breeders. A really sick foal who cannot get up can be covered with a blanket or an electric blanket (provided the heat is monitored). Whatever measures are taken to keep the foal warm, its rectal temperature should be taken at hourly intervals to ensure the temperature is being maintained at 38.5°C (100.5°F). If the foal's temperature is higher or lower than this appropriate measures need to be taken to cool or warm the foal.

Bright lights should be avoided when nursing a sick foal, although if these are needed for veterinary procedures then obviously they should be used. Otherwise you can do little more than provide tender loving care and a warm, draught-free stable. Provided you take heed of all instructions left by the veterinary surgeon you can rest assured all that can be done for your foal is being done.

AILMENTS AND DISEASE IN THE FOAL

It is the veterinary surgeon's job to diagnose diseases in the foal, but it is your responsibility to observe the very first signs of any disease so that the veterinary surgeon may be called without delay. What follows is not intended to replace veterinary advice, but it will help you to make an educated assessment of your foal's health.

Meconium retention

Meconium is the faecal matter that has accumulated in the foal's intestines before birth. While the foal is still in the womb this matter does not pose any threat to the foal, but once the foal is born it is essential that it is disposed of as quickly as possible or else it will start to have a toxic effect. Unlike droppings from milk or grass, meconium is a very dark greeny-black in colour. Most foals pass the meconium quite easily and quickly, and you should observe the foal within the first few hours of birth to ensure this is happening. You can be sure the meconium has completely passed out of the body when the faecal matter turns paler as the milk from its dam starts to come through. It is quite dangerous to assume that this has happened without actually observing it, as meconium retention can prove fatal within a short space of time. It is not enough simply to observe that 'some' meconium has been passed as there are a few inches to be disposed of. The critical point is that it changes colour, indicating that fresh faeces are passing through the whole of the intestines.

The first sign that meconium has been retained is that the foal stops suckling. To be sure it has stopped, you will have to try to observe the foal unnoticed as it may be less inclined to feed in your presence. However, foals usually suckle for comfort if they have been unsettled, perhaps by having people in the stable, so leave the stable as normal, but quietly observe through a peep-hole or similar if possible, as this will give you a true measure of the foal's actions. If the foal does not suckle then, and continues not to do so, you can be sure there is a problem and you should call the vet.

As time goes by the foal will stand with his tail lifted as if expecting to pass something, but nothing is seen. Progression of the condition will see the foal straining to pass faeces but without success and then the development of colic-type symptoms, such as rolling about and laying its head back along its abdomen. The more the condition goes untreated the more toxic the foal gets and the worse it becomes. Without feed the foal will become weaker and, if the condition is left unresolved, it may die in quite a miserable state.

Fig. 70 A foal straining to pass meconium will stand in this crouched position repeatedly.

The best treatment for meconium retention is to try to prevent it in the first place. The first thing you can do is to ensure the foal suckles within the first hour or two of birth as the dam's colostrum has a laxative effect. If the foal is weak, or is having trouble, you should help it to suckle. If you do this for the first few times, he will then gain strength and have the inclination to suckle for himself. If, despite suckling soon after birth, the foal still 'goes off suck' you may be able to clear the blockage manually by inserting the tip of a well-lubricated little finger carefully into the rectum, to see if there is simply a lump of meconium stuck in the passage. This must be done extremely carefully as the tissues in the rectum are very sensitive and fragile. Do not try to reach in further than the knuckle joint of your little finger otherwise you may damage the foal. If this does not solve the problem, and quickly, you must call the vet as there is no more you can do. In the majority of cases the vet is able to clear the blockage by giving the foal an enema. If this does not work, the vet will probably refer the foal to an equine hospital where the blockage may need to be flushed out by means of a stomach tube or, in rarer cases, by surgery. Colts are more commonly affected by meconium retention than fillies and when affected they are often more troublesome to remedy than fillies.

To recap, most foals have passed their meconium by the end of the second or, at the latest, third day after birth. By the fourth day they should certainly be passing milk-dung. It is also a good idea to note whether urine is being passed as this is one of the signs that will help the vet decide whether the condition is in fact retained meconium: failure to pass urine may indicate a ruptured bladder. If you are in any doubt about whether or not your foal is suffering from these ailments, do not delay – call the vet.

Ruptured bladder

A ruptured bladder needs immediate veterinary attention. If your foal has passed meconium, but is still straining and showing signs that the abdomen is starting to fill, call the vet without delay. Other major abnormalities in the gut will cause acute signs of colic at between twelve and twenty-four hours after birth, and again the vet needs to attend immediately to offer a diagnosis.

Diarrhoea

Diarrhoea in foals is commonly known as 'scouring', and it is a symptom of a number of diseases, rather than a disease in itself. It may be very insignificant, or it may be a vital sign that all is not well. The most common reason for scouring is that the dam has come into season. This being the case the foal may scour at between seven and fourteen days after birth. No treatment is needed although vigilance is required to ensure the condition clears up quickly. If it does not the foal may have a secondary ailment. Upon noticing your foal scouring you should note the following information for the veterinary surgeon:

- Whether or not the dam is in season.
- The foal's temperature.
- The colour of the faeces.
- Whether the foal is feeding normally or is 'off-suck'.
- The appearance and feel of the mucous

membranes, which should be moist and a normal salmon-pink colour, but may be pale and dry, or displaying some other abnormal characteristics.
• The appearance and feel of the tongue, which should be moist and pink, but may be dry, furry or slimy.
• The smell of the faeces: odourless, foul or mild smelling.
• The consistency of the faeces: like water, pasty, slimy or lumpy.
• The colour of the faeces: pale, green, brown or grey.
• The overall appearance and behaviour of the foal: normal or hyper-active or listless and uninterested.
• Whether the foal is drinking lots of water.

In any event it is a good idea to take a sample of the faeces to give to the veterinary surgeon for analysis. If an infection is suspected the dam and foal will need to be isolated from other horses in the yard. Diarrhoea can be extremely serious so do not delay in getting a veterinary opinion.

Rotavirus

Rotavirus is one of the ailments that can cause bad diarrhoea and as its name suggests it is a viral infection. Its presence can easily be confirmed by a faecal sample. Other symptoms, such as lethargy, colic-type pains and fever, may also be present so speedy veterinary treatment is essential.

Eye problems

Occasionally foals may suffer from runny eyes. The most usual cause is entropion, a condition causing the lower eyelid to slant inwards so that the fine hairs rub against the surface of the eye. If you can see that this is what is causing the problem, your foal will need a small operation which involves removing a slither of skin below the eye to pull the lower lid outwards into its natural place. Obviously this procedure must only be undertaken by a veterinary surgeon. If you are sure that entropion is not the problem you should still have the vet check your foal to determine the cause of the runny eyes.

Umbilical Hernia

This is a very common condition in foals, and it is caused by a weakness of the abdominal wall. Hernias do not become apparent until the foal is about four weeks old, but the good news is that most hernias disappear without trace, although larger ones will need veterinary attention. If you feel the hernia you will find that it can all be pushed back up into the foal's body and may admit one or two fingers. As the foal grows the opening closes, but larger hernias may need a small operation, so you need to have the vet advise you on the best course of treatment.

When the foal is more than four months old an elastrator ring (the sort applied to lambs' tails) is put onto the 'sac' of the hernia, but this must only be done in the knowledge that the contents of the hernia itself have been absorbed back into the abdomen. Otherwise a section of intestines may become trapped and cause severe colic, or prove fatal. Once the elastrator ring has been applied, the middle of the hernia will close up within a month, and the trapped and unwanted skin will simply drop off. This is not some-

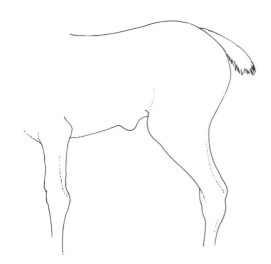

Fig. 71 Umbilical hernia.

thing that should be done without veterinary attention, and the foal will need to be covered for tetanus before doing so.

Bent legs

Bent legs at birth are extremely common and often the foal looks quite deformed. However, within hours or days the legs strengthen and soon they take on their correct appearance. However, there may be times when the foal's bent legs are a little more serious requiring corrective treatment.

Growth plates are sites at the ends of bones where most of the bone growth takes place. Bent legs are caused by one side of the growth plate on the forelegs growing faster than the other side, either on the inside or the outside from either the knee or fetlock. 'Valgus' is the term used for legs bent outwards and 'varus' for legs that are bent inwards. So a knee that is bent outwards is termed 'Carpal valgus' and this is the most common deformity in foals,

making them appear to be knock-kneed.

Provided the foal is neither overweight nor hyperactive, such limbs will straighten of their own accord. Whether or not they will straighten back to normal is a matter for veterinary assessment, and box rest may be advised in the early stages. The vet may also advise that you have a farrier trim and balance the feet sooner than normal to help encourage correct growth.

Before the growth plates stop growing a decision needs to be taken as to whether surgery will be needed because after the plates stop growing it will be too late to do anything. Counterbalancing the rate of growth on each side of the leg can be performed surgically and this is usually successful, although it is thought that such a foal may be predisposed to arthritis in later life.

Joint problems

Joint problems in foals are usually caused by injuries or stresses of one kind or another. Few foals are born with 'bad joints' (although in some cases there may be some hereditary susceptibility). Stresses can be caused by knocks or bangs, or just as much by a bad diet, which in turn may cause physitis (swelling at the joints). Obviously, to a great extent it is impossible to protect a foal from every knock, but care should be taken not to allow the foal to become overweight or malnourished.

Hind limb deformities

The most common hind limb deformity is known as 'down on its fetlocks', and as the name implies this means that the fetlocks are near to the floor. While this condition usually gets better on its own as the legs strengthen, the fetlocks may need to be bandaged to protect them from rubbing on the floor.

Flexural deformities

These are seen in rapidly growing foals and are quite painful. The foal is seen to take all its weight on the toes of the hoof, so it looks as though the foal is walking on tip toes. Treatment needs be quite drastic in that the diet must be reduced dramatically. The farrier can then adjust the feet, perhaps by fitting a toe extension so that the foal is encouraged to take more weight on its heels as normal. In severe cases that do not respond to such measures the check ligament may need to be cut in order that the flexor tendon can stretch.

9 Care of the Mare and Foal

THE FIRST FEW DAYS

Your mare will introduce herself to her new foal with little whickers and whinnies and by nuzzling it. Some mares take a little time to get used to the idea of being a mum, especially if they are maidens, so do not be too disappointed if she does not seem to want to know her foal straight away.

After a little rest, your mare will get up and start to lick her foal in order to dry its coat and so prevent chilling. If she shows no inclination to do this, then you should get some clean dry towels and briskly rub the foal over yourself (*see* page 83).

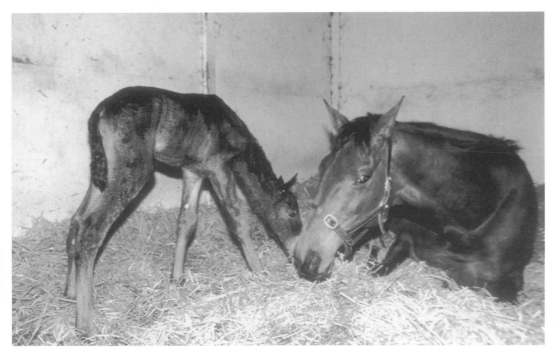

Fig. 72 Your mare will introduce herself to her foal with little whickers and whinnies.

The suckling foal

Most foals will get up and start to suckle within a few hours of birth and as long as all seems well you should not interfere with the process. Waiting for a foal to feed can be extremely frustrating. It will make endless attempts, only to 'miss' the target each time. However, eventually the foal does find the teat and after the first suck there is usually no stopping it. Occasionally, foals do fail to find the teat, and in such cases it is a good idea to give them a little helping hand before they become too tired. Have someone hold your mare and gently guide the foal by placing an arm around its quarters, towards your mare's udder. Gently squeeze the teat so that a few drops of milk are produced and push the foal's head towards it. If the foal

seems to have no inclination to suck, you should open its mouth and place the teat between its lips, squeezing out some drops of milk at the same time. Usually the smell, and taste of the milk, is enough to trigger the foal's sucking mechanism. Once the foal has sucked naturally for the first time it will continue to do so, finding the udder on its own, so further help should not be required.

If the foal is so weak that it cannot get up to suck, you will have to milk the colostrum from your mare and give it to the foal by means of a feeding bottle. You can use a baby's feeding bottle and a rubber calf's or lamb's teat for the job. It is essential that the foal takes in the colostrum as this contains many of the antibodies that will help to protect it during the first few weeks of its vulnerable

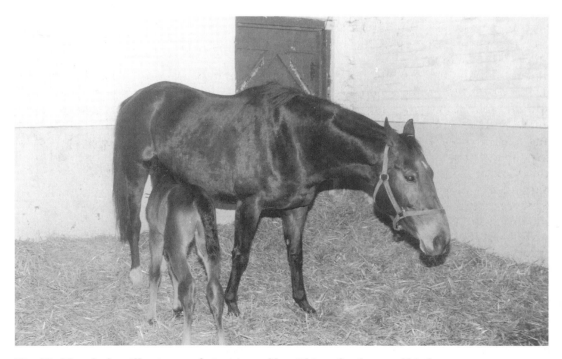

Fig. 73 Most foals will get up and start to suckle within a few hours of birth.

life. At first the foal will be able to take only small amounts of colostrum, so you will have to feed it at two-hourly intervals. However, after a couple of feeds it should be strong enough to suckle itself and the sooner you can get it back on to its mother the better. Once a foal has learned to suck from a bottle it is very difficult to get it back onto the teat, so immediately the foal begins to suck (as opposed to your squeezing small amounts of colostrum into its mouth) then you should encourage it to return to its mother.

The foal slip

Foals run instinctively, so it will not take your foal long to find its feet. You should put on a foal slip, or small adjustable headcollar, as soon as possible within the first forty-eight hours of birth. This will ensure you can catch the foal and hold it securely when necessary. A foal slip also allows you to lead the foal, which is preferable to leaving it following its dam. In preparation for fitting a foal slip, you should accustom your foal to being touched. Run your hands all over its body and caress behind its ears, talking to it all the time so that it becomes used to your voice. A very young foal can damage its neck if it panics and tries to pull away while the slip is being held, so the foal should first be taught to lead by use of a stable rubber around its neck and a guiding arm around the quarters. Once the foal accepts going forwards with you, the foal slip can be introduced. The easiest way to do this is to back the foal into a corner of the stable. Stand on the foal's near side and holding the slip in your left hand, place your right arm over the foal's neck. Grasp the foal slip on either side of

the noseband, then gently but swiftly ease it up over the muzzle and quickly fasten the headpiece on the near side. This lesson can be repeated daily until the foal shows no concern. Whether you leave the foaling slip on constantly is a matter of personal preference. I do, as it enables you to get hold of the foal quickly in any event. However, even when the foal slip is left on constantly, it should still be removed and put back on daily to teach the foal acceptance of it and handling of his head. In any case, the foal slip needs to be kept clean and supple so that it does not cause any sores. The foal must learn to accept you holding the slip, and should not be allowed to pull away from you. A guiding arm around the quarters while the foal is still small should help it to understand that pressure on the slip means walk forwards.

Turning out

Provided it is clear and dry on the day following the birth your mare and foal will benefit from being turned out and will continue to thrive if kept outdoors. Obviously precautions such as ensuring the fencing is safe, and that there is no rubbish in the field, should be taken.

THE FIRST FEW WEEKS

Your foal will sleep a great deal in the first few weeks of life, but as it grows it will become quite inquisitive. Whenever you walk into the field or stable the foal will look towards you, and it is then that you will feel a great sense of pride; it is also at this time that you start to wonder whether

Fig. 74 Foals run instinctively, so it is a good idea to put on a foal slip as soon as possible after birth in case you need to catch the foal in a hurry.

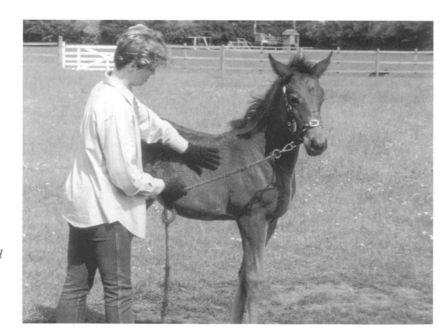

Fig. 75 It is a good idea to get the foal used to being touched and handled on a regular basis.

Fig. 76 Safe fencing is a must when turning out newly born foals. Note that the hedge behind acts as a visible barrier.

another foal (just as a playmate of course!) might be a good idea.

Provided your mare allows you to handle the foal without signs of stress, you can weigh the foal soon after birth. Bring an ordinary pair of bathroom scales into the stable and site them on a bare, flat surface. Then stand on the scales yourself to determine your own weight. Once you have done this have someone help you lift the foal into your arms while you remain on the scales. Deduct your own weight and you will be able to see exactly how much the foal weighs. You can then keep assessing the foal's weight during the following days and first weeks until it is simply too heavy for you to hold. This will give you peace of mind: if the foal is putting on weight it means that it is getting enough nourishment.

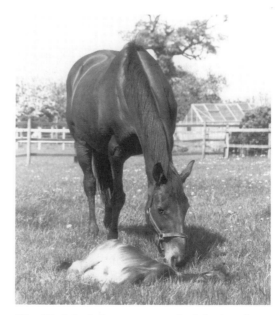

Fig. 77 A foal sleeps a great deal during the first few weeks of life, and during this time mum keeps a watchful eye over him.

101

Supplementing the mare's milk

The foal will be provided with nearly all necessary nourishment from his mother's milk, and as he grows will find most of what he needs in good grazing. However, nutrients in the mother's milk decline as lactation continues, and if the foal does not have access to excellent pasture he will need creep feeding. The term 'creep' describes an enclosure where the foal, but not the mare, can gain access to the feed put down. There are now specially designed 'creep' feeders on the market. Creep feeding can begin from about three weeks onwards.

Care needs to be taken not to over- nor to underfeed the foal, so he should be kept away from the mother's ration. Overeating can lead to rapid growth, which enhances the possibility of the foal developing metabolic bone disease.

The easiest way to ensure your foal gets all it needs is to use a proprietary brand of properly formulated feed that is designed to be fed alongside the mare's milk and grass. In this way you can be sure the foal is obtaining the correct supply of minerals, vitamins and protein, along with adequate calcium, phosphorous and trace minerals needed for good bone growth.

Every day a foal should consume 450g (1lb) for each month of his life. So at three months of age he will be having 1.36kg (3lb) of food (*see* also Chapter 10).

What must be avoided is providing too

Fig. 78 A foal is provided with all the necessary nutrients from its mother's milk.

Fig. 79 A specially designed creep-feeder to prevent the foal's dam from taking its food.

Fig. 80 Likewise the foal should be kept away from its mother's rations!

much digestible energy so the foal simply puts on weight rather than quality growth. Excess weight puts strain on the developing bones and joints, often resulting in problems. Youngsters that are forced on in such a way for the show ring, or for the Thoroughbred racing sales, can often suffer in this way.

Worming

Certain worms can be passed to foals through the mare's milk, so it is important to ensure your mare is correctly wormed before foaling (*see* Chapter 4). If a young foal does suffer from worms he may quickly develop diarrhoea and become ill. A foal is susceptible to the same worms that trouble adult horses, although he may also be at risk from the large round-worm. Older horses develop an immunity against this worm, but in the young foal infestation can prove fatal.

The best course of action is to ensure your paddocks are as worm-free as possible. This means picking up drop-pings and ensuring a correct worming programme for all horses grazing the land.

The foal's feet

At birth the foal comes into the world with a white, flaky protective covering on its hooves which is designed to protect the internal organs of the mare. This usually sloughs off within twenty-four hours of birth and the hoof takes on a normal

Fig. 81 Correct farriery is essential for the developing foal, and a farrier who is experienced with youngstock is required.

appearance. It is most desirable that the foal's legs are handled as soon as possible after birth as lessons and trust learnt in the first few days of life will always be remembered. Be careful not to 'hang on' to your foal's legs, but lift them gently, allowing the hoof to rest in the palm of your hand. In this way the foal does not feel trapped and you will not damage sensitive structures by restraining them should the foal pull his hoof away. During the first few weeks of life the tissues of the feet are still relatively soft, so do not be tempted to pick them out as you would an older horse. If something does become lodged between the frog and hoof wall try to pick it out with your fingers before resorting to a gently manoeuvred hoof pick.

Any limb deformities at birth should be noted. If remedial work is required the sooner the vet and farrier start a corrective plan of action the better. Even quite bad lower limb deformities can be rectified if caught soon enough.

At two months of age a foal should start to have his feet trimmed. It is essential to have a farrier who is experienced with youngstock carry out this job: just as deformities can be cured, so can they be caused by bad trimming. The quality of the horn of the hoof itself is dependent on good feeding and, as the greater part of the foal's diet comes from the mare, no additives should be necessary at this young age. Once the foal is weaned, however, he may require extra calcium in his diet to help both bone and horn growth. In the first year of his life the foal's feet should be trimmed up every four to six weeks and picked out on a daily basis.

As the time for first shoes approaches the youngster should have his feet lightly tapped and his leg held between yours to accustom him to the work the farrier has to perform – remember, it is your job to train your foal, not the farrier's.

NUTRITION IN THE LACTATING MARE

It used to be normal practice to give the mare a bran mash as soon as she had foaled. *Do not* do this. Bran is highly indigestible and causes problems of calcium uptake. The newly foaled mare requires more calcium than ever for lactation, so giving her a bran mash is the last thing you should do. You should simply offer her a small feed of what she is used to with a good amount of sugar beet in it.

Before discussing the feed your mare will require, it cannot be stressed enough the importance of providing a plentiful supply of fresh, clean water. Your mare will also require more salt in her diet than normal, up to four tablespoons a day for a 500kg (10cwt) mare. You will have to check the manufacturer's guidelines on the bags of feed that you use to see how much salt there is in the feed, otherwise call them and ask. If the quantity of salt is not enough you will have to supplement it yourself. However, you will not go far wrong if you stick to a reputable brand of formulated stud mix, or cubes, together with good spring grass.

A lactating mare will require a higher quantity of feed than when she was pregnant. Her diet should satisfy all of her protein, energy, mineral and vitamin needs (especially folic acid which can easily become deficient after foaling). Her protein and energy requirements will rise to 14 per cent crude protein of her total diet in the first three months of lactation. Thereafter they reduce to 12 per cent until the foal is weaned, when they will return to her pre-pregnancy levels.

Whatever type of feed you choose, you must:

1. Provide adequate levels of fibre.
2. Ensure the stability of the gut's micro-organisms.

The best form of fibre is of course grass, but if supplies are not adequate at the time of year that your mare foals you should supply ad lib hay. The micro-organisms in the gut play a vital role in the health of both mare and foal. To ensure these remain as stable as possible do not play around with your mare's diet. It should be kept constant, and the feeds should be split into three feeds a day, or a minimum of two if this is not possible; and the addition of chaff to each feed is a good idea.

You can only be guided by the condition of your own mare, but as a rough guide you should supply feed as follows:

• For the first three months of lactation: 45 per cent forage, 55 per cent concentrates, at 3kg (6lb 10oz) per 100kg (220lb) of bodyweight. For example a 500kg (10cwt) mare will require 15kg (33lb) a day.
• Post three months lactation to weaning of foal: 60 per cent forage to 40 per cent concentrates, at 2.5kg (5lb 8oz) per 100kg (220lb) of bodyweight. Poor doers may need to stay on 3kg (6lb 10oz) per 100kg (220lb) of bodyweight.
• After weaning: 75 per cent forage to 25 per cent concentrates, at 2.5kg (5lb 8oz) per 100kg (220lb) bodyweight.

10 Weaning

PREPARATION

As the time for weaning approaches, your foal should be on full daily concentrate rations, coupled with good grass or quality alternative forage. This ensures the foal will not be set back by the change of diet during weaning. When the foal is three months of age, and is grazing well, the mare's concentrates should be reduced (*see* Chapter 9), and the foal's increased. This will help the mare's milk to dry up more quickly and will encourage the foal to eat the alternative feed more readily. Five days before weaning it is a good idea to introduce probiotics to the foal's diet in order to minimize stress and help to prevent scouring after weaning. These should be continued until five days after weaning.

Fig. 82 As the time for weaning approaches the foal should be on full daily concentrate rations.

Fig. 83 Before deciding to wean take a good look at the condition of your foal. This foal is nicely covered and, at six months old, is ready to leave its mother. However, a smaller, weaker, or thinner, foal will need longer with its mother if weaning is not to prove too stressful.

HOW TO WEAN

There are various ways to wean foals, one of which you will have to choose to suit your individual requirements.

This first method is a complete separation of mare and foal on a given day, at a given time. Usually the mare is walked out of the stable and the foal is shut up behind the door. This is very traumatic for both mare and foal and usually there is a lot of neighing and calling. Provided the mare is taken completely out of sight and earshot the foal will settle down within a few days. If using this method of weaning, you should take care when first you turn the foal out into the paddock as it may

decide to go looking for its dam, forgetting that fences are there to keep it in. It is sensible to have another playmate in the field to divert the foal's attention and offer comfort. In some circumstances it may be possible to introduce a playmate into the stable at the point of weaning. Another newly weaned foal is ideal for the job as both will feel vulnerable and will therefore cling to each other for comfort rather than one taking a dominant stance against the other. If another weanling cannot be found then a docile pony, or horse can be used as a substitute. However, closely observe the pair in the stable to ensure no bullying is taking place. It is quite normal for two usually placid horses to take a dislike to each other, and so their association in such close quarters will not benefit either of them. Plenty of small feeds should be offered to either the lone foal, or the pair in the stable, to distract their attention and keep them occupied. Once they appear settled, they can be turned out together. Provided they are quite amicable towards each other, two weanlings can happily share the same stable over the winter months.

The second method is that of gradual weaning, and this is my preferred method. A group of mares and foals are introduced to each other in a paddock (although I have also used this method with older

Fig. 84 Bye, bye mum! One method of weaning is simply to separate mare and foal on a given day.

horses, geldings and mares, together with foals). Once the group has sorted out its hierarchy one mare can be quickly and quietly removed. Preferably this should be the dam of the most independent, and most mature, foal. This dam should be put out of earshot, or if this is not possible she should be put into a separate, non-adjoining field with another companion. Over a period of days, the rest of the mares can be removed (provided, of course, their foals are all ready to be weaned) one at a time, to the other paddock containing the mares already moved. Some people tend to leave the mare of the youngest foal with the group, however, I have not found this necessary, and have found that a placid two or three year old serves just as well as a 'guardian' over the winter. Even an older, gentle gelding can take on this role without detriment to the group of youngsters.

WEANLING ALONE

How should you go about weaning a foal if there are no companions with whom he can share the experience? Suddenly separating mare and foal, leaving the foal alone in his own company, is traumatic for both and can cause a lasting sense of insecurity in the foal. To avoid this, gradual weaning can take place over a period of weeks. To begin with, this will involve erecting a safe barrier in the loose-box; the mare can then be put on one side and the foal on the other. Both will be able to see and hear each other, but the foal will not be able to suckle. At first, an hour's separation will be sufficient. As their acceptance of the barrier grows, the periods of separation can be lengthened over the following weeks until the foal is living permanently in the 'stable' next to its dam.

However, this will not complete the weaning process because as soon as mare and foal are released together into a paddock the foal will undoubtedly resume suckling. It will therefore be necessary to turn them out separately. Having become accustomed to living with the barrier between them, each should be turned out for half a day and then brought back in before the other is turned out for the remainder of the day. The foal will gradually become used to being alone for periods, although while he is in the paddock a watchful eye will be needed to make sure he does not try to jump out. You will need to continue this separate turning out for at least three months, but even after this period you will still need to be vigilant in case the foal attempts to suckle again.

For the mare owner who has simply bred one foal and does not intend to breed another – at least for some time – it is questionable whether weaning is necessary at all. In my opinion it is not necessary to wean a foal if the mare is not in foal again. I have left mare and foal together for three years and allowed nature to take its course. The mare's milk dried up after about nine months and gradually the foal became more independent. As a three-year-old that foal is the most lovely tempered horse: she mixes easily with others and is extremely well

Fig. 85 A group of newly weaned foals soon settles down to life without mum.

Fig. 86 Other placid horses can serve as guardians over the winter months, and provided there are no bullies in the field the group will soon sort out its hierarchy.

behaved when handled. So weaning is all about facilities and finding a solution that suits the individual best. It is not something that has to be accomplished at all costs.

AFTERCARE OF THE MARE

Some mares react very little to the weaning process, almost as though they are glad to be rid of their burden; others fret for days. Apart from providing suitable companions, there is little you can do to ease the stress for the mare, but most do settle within forty-eight hours of weaning. However, there are some practical considerations such as ensuring the mare is not on lush grass. The aim is to stop her production of milk as soon as possible and this will not happen if she is gorging on lush grass. Ideally she should be put into a fairly sparse paddock to reduce the quality of her diet.

Milk should not be drawn off the mare as this only encourages the production of more. However, you must check to ensure that her udder is not becoming hard, lumpy or too painful. A certain amount of discomfort is inevitable, but real pain is a sign that mastitis is developing and so veterinary attention will be required (*see* page 85). After two weeks the udder should have reduced considerably in size and the mare's rations can be gradually increased to normal.

111

NUTRITION IN THE WEANLING

The most important part of a youngster's routine is feed times, and these should be as regular as possible. Ideally, a weanling should be fed two or three times a day, but where this is not possible it is even more important to ensure that feed is provided at a specific time. The young horse is totally in our control as far as what he eats goes, so we must provide him with a suitably balanced diet, relevant to each stage of his growth.

Fig. 87 The most important part of a young-ster's routine is feeding time, which should be kept as regular as possible two or three times a day.

The youngster does most of his growing as a weanling. He will attain about 80 per cent of his full adult height during this period and should be fed accordingly, but he must be allowed plenty of exercise too. As the youngster matures, his protein and energy requirements decrease, although he must still have adequate levels of each if he is to mature correctly. As he grows, his roughage can be increased and his concentrates slightly reduced.

Throughout, it is much safer to stick to one really good brand of rearing diet and follow qualified advice, as ongoing research throws up new evidence and things change rapidly. As a result, feed formulations change and your youngster will therefore still receive a balanced ration.

COLTS

Colts do not usually require any extra management until they are nearing their first birthday. This probably coincides with mares' coming into season and so the arousal of the colt's sexual behaviour. It is also thought that perfume can have a similar effect on colts, so you should be aware of this when handling them. Colts do need strict handling if they are to be manageable. They must not be allowed to rear up on the lead line, or to 'play' with you when in the field. Some owners take great delight in playing 'tag' with their colts in the field, only then to wonder why the colt goes for them, or kicks them. If you act like a playmate, you will receive rough – but to him natural – treatment, so this is a grave mistake. At all costs colts must learn to respect their handlers from day one, especially if they are to be kept entire.

Gelding

Colts are castrated for various reasons. The most obvious is so that they can be kept in the same paddock as mares. Other reasons include making them easier and more docile to handle, and preventing unwanted pregnancies.

The optimum time for castration will be dictated by the individual colt's maturity, age, behaviour, and physical development. A colt that is considered to be puny may be left entire for up to eighteen months in order that he develops a better top-line. Obviously this is only an option if he is not grazed with mares and will receive knowledgeable, confident handling. However, colts are not usually castrated before five months of age, although around this time the process is less traumatic than it is for the older horse. In general, colts are castrated at about a year old. This usually coincides with the start of the spring, which tends to move most people to have colts castrated. Castration at this time prevents much of the 'colty' behaviour that would otherwise be displayed, but it is important that the operation is carried out before the onset of the fly season: castration results in an open wound and the last thing that is needed is infection by flies.

Although the thought of castration is not a pleasant one the process is routine and usually without complications. The scrotum is opened and cut, and the spermatic cord crushed to prevent bleeding. Castration may be carried out 'standing', whereby the horse is tranquillized and castrated under local anaesthetic; 'in the field', whereby the horse is anaesthetized and left to come round in the field; or 'in the theatre', although this is usually recommended only if complications are thought likely to arise or if there is a known problem.

After castration care must be taken of the colt. He may swell up quite a lot and be in some discomfort. Your job is to try to keep flies away from the wound and to keep the youngster as quiet as possible. If it is warm and flies are a problem he will have to be kept in a stable, although this is not advantageous as exercise helps to reduce the swelling. Similarly if he thrashes about the field, which is not usual but sometimes happens, you will have to keep him stabled for the first few days.

11 Care and Training of the Youngster

NUTRITION IN THE YOUNG HORSE

The nutritional needs of the foal and weanling have been dealt with in Chapters 9 and 10 respectively, but how about the yearling and older youngster? As a yearling the horse must not be allowed to become too fat or too thin, otherwise problems of growth can occur. As a yearling we should be looking to promote a steady and slow growth rate, which is achieved through the winter by feeding 40 to 60 per cent roughage with smaller quantities of concentrates. During the spring the best thing you can do is to turn the yearling out on to good grazing, as this will supply him with all his nutritional needs. It is vitally important that the yearling is not overfed. The yearling's frame needs time to grow and mature, without the restriction of too much fat. At this stage in a horse's life many more developmental problems occur from over-feeding rather than from under-feeding. As with all aspects of horse management, the yearling must be treated individually. If he is becoming too fat, his diet must be modified by replacing some of his concen-

trates with good-quality forage. If his diet is purely good spring grass, his access to it will have to be curtailed for periods of the day.

As the horse matures his feeding requirements change. His diet will need to be considered in the light of his size, body-weight, breed and condition. So a 13hh. Welsh pony will need to be assessed differently from a 16.2hh. Thoroughbred. The first thing is to ensure a good supply of quality hay is always on offer throughout the winter months. A balanced supply of concentrates selected according to the above factors will then need to be supplied.

If you are in any doubt about what to feed you can call the helpline of any of the major feed companies who will be happy to discuss your individual requirements. The numbers of these are usually to be found in national horse magazines.

STABLING OR GRASS?

Should a young horse be stabled or left to 'harden up' over its first winter? This question often causes much debate amongst breeders. On the one hand there are those that feel horses should live in conditions as near as possible to their natural environment. On the other, there are those that feel a horse will only thrive if he endures no hardship. Your own decision should be made in consideration of the facilities you have available. I do believe that it is good for a horse to live in his natural environment, but we must remember that many horses are no longer 'natural' animals. They have been domesticated and finely bred for our own use and it is obvious that no finely bred horse should be turned out over the winter to fend for himself. The ideal for any horse is a paddock with good shelter, safe fencing, clean water facilities, the company of other horses, and an adequate supply of supplementary food. The fewer of these facilities you have the more you will have to make adjustments to the routine: if your field does not have shelter you will have to stable your horse overnight, and if the weather turns particularly nasty, you will have to rug him up if he is a fine breed. There can be no compromise on safe fencing, fresh water and an adequate supply of food, meaning ad lib hay and sufficient concentrates for his needs. Companionship should also not be underestimated. A youngster, especially, needs to learn to be part of a group and to fit into a social structure. A youngster kept outdoors as much as possible in this way is far less likely to develop dust allergies and/or stable vices.

EMOTIONAL NEEDS

A horse's emotional needs may seem a strange thing to consider, as we cannot always know for certain what a horse really wants or feels. But it is impossible to rear and train a young horse to the best of his ability if he is unhappy; and so every effort must be made to understand and respond to his state of mind. While we cannot know what is in the horse's mind we do have a gauge against which to judge his emotional needs, and that is his temperament. As we saw in the early chapters, to a certain extent his temperament is inherited from either one or both parents. At first a foal may simply be copying the dam's behaviour, but as he matures his own personality, likes and dislikes, will develop. An important factor that affects the horse's mind is the environment in which he lives. As far as the young horse is concerned the less restrictive his environment the better. It therefore follows that many of the temperamental difficulties of youngsters are man-made. If you lock a youngster up in a stable all day he is bound to become fretful, which may manifest itself in either miserable or over-zealous behaviour. Of course all horses have their own individual personalities and some are naturally more laid-back or fizzy than others. However, it is the responsibility of anyone who breeds his own youngster to find out just what it is that makes him 'tick' and, equipped with this knowledge, to provide the necessary stimulus to satisfy each individual's needs.

HANDLING AND TEACHING BASIC MANNERS

Deciding to train a young horse is an enormous undertaking. The process can bring immense satisfaction if you are successful, but if you are not the youngster may be left with problems for the rest of his life, so think very carefully before you make any decisions. Training a youngster takes commitment and dedication. It is not a job to be rushed and there is no set pattern to follow as every horse needs to be treated as an individual. When educating the young horse, the aim is to produce a sensible, well-balanced and willing companion who has faith in those who handle and ride him. He should be confident in responding to all that you ask of him and, through correct management in his early years, should never be allowed to believe that he can take advantage of you, or anyone else.

Correct early education lays a sound foundation from which a horse will develop further. Any amount of training will not produce a brilliant performer if the horse is simply not athletic enough or does not have the right temperament; you can only bring out what natural abilities the horse may have.

Starting with the right horse is of paramount importance, as the job is made twice as hard if you have to deal with a difficult character. Having bred the horse yourself, you will be able to handle him from the start, by gently stroking him and talking to him within a few hours of birth.

Fig. 88 Through correct handling in the early months, a foal learns that he cannot take advantage of you.

By starting with so young an animal, with correct management you will be able to instil confidence and understanding from the beginning, which will help immensely when it comes to training sessions. A horse's first year is a time of playfulness. He will experiment and explore, and unless he is handled firmly at this age problems can develop. It is natural for a horse to bite and kick. Just watch two yearlings in the field to see this sort of behaviour at its best! So it is at this time when you will need to teach your youngster respect for you and others who may handle him.

The voice

Your voice plays a very important role in successfully educating your youngster. Used quietly and soothingly it will encourage him and promote confidence in him. Raising the tone, as opposed to shouting which serves little purpose, conveys the message that some sort of correction is needed in his behaviour.

The voice is the one thing throughout the training period that remains constant. Your horse will have become accustomed to your voice throughout his early handling, and will have learnt what

Fig. 89 Having bred the foal yourself you will be able to handle it from the start, and take it out and about to increase its confidence in new situations.

117

Punishment and Reward

The most successful way of dealing with youngsters of any age is to adopt a system of punishment and reward. They soon learn that reward follows correct behaviour and punishment follows undesirable behaviour. Punishment or reward must be immediate and appropriate if it is to be clear to the horse that he has behaved well or unacceptably. Withholding reward is in itself a punishment and, in this way, the horse does not become frightened or nervous when he does something wrong, but seeks to do as we ask in search of reward. The misuse of punishment in early training is one of the worst errors that can be made. By doing so, a friendly, willing and confident animal can be reduced to a permanently timid, anxious and distrustful horse.

Fig. 90 The reward of a handful of grass soon teaches this foal to stand still when required.

certain words mean by the tone you use when giving verbal instructions. This is extremely useful when it comes to lungeing and long-reining (*see* Chapter 12). A few basic words completely understood by the horse will enable you to manoeuvre him without confusion.

Key words are: 'Walk-on' which is said in a light, brisk tone; 'Whooa', in a low soothing tone to let the horse know to slow down as desired; and finally 'StanD' with the d emphasized. The horse also learns very quickly to respond to 'Good boy/girl' by relaxing and to 'No' by paying more attention. It is also a good idea to frequently call your horse by name, as this will let him know you are talking to him when he is around other horses. Other useful words are 'Over', when asking the horse to move away from you in the stable, and 'Give it up' when asking him to lift his feet. (As training progresses you may use 'Tr-rot!' which is said in a slightly higher tone to encourage the horse to trot on and 'Canter-up' which is said in a light, brisk tone slightly higher than to trot on.)

With these few key words understood, you will have a horse who is well mannered in the stable, will walk on and stand when in hand, and will respond to instructions when beginning his training.

Actions

The horse does not respond so well to actions, especially if given without a verbal command, except of course in the case of the ridden horse where he learns to respond to his rider's aids.

However, any physical instructions that are given, such as laying a hand on the horse in the stable to encourage him to move over, should be light and clear. A great slap is not necessary. Contrary to popular belief the horse does not like to be patted strongly. If you teach the horse to respond to light handling from the beginning he will never need anything stronger. If something goes wrong you should not be quick to blame the horse, but look towards

Fig. 91 As training progresses you may teach the word 'Tr-r-ot!', said in a light tone to encourage the youngster to trot on command.

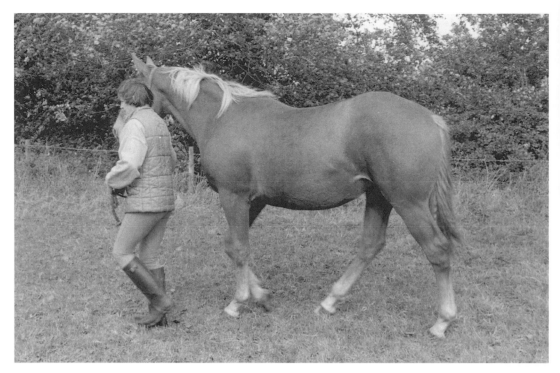

Fig. 92 Once a youngster has learnt to lead correctly, he can be expected to obey you when asked to walk anywhere you require.

your own actions first. Did you try to ask too much? Did you ask clearly enough? Is the horse tired? Are you tired? You should always give your horse the benefit of the doubt. If you are satisfied that your actions are correct you should then ask the horse to respond again before taking any disciplinary action.

It never pays to pick an argument with a horse unnecessarily. When teaching the youngster to lead in hand, why ask him to lead away from his pals, when he will happily obey you if you ask him to lead towards them? Once he knows what leading is, then he can be expected to obey you further by walking away when asked.

You should always be certain the horse

is capable of doing what you ask, both physically and mentally.

PRACTICAL TRAINING: THE FIRST YEAR

The education of any horse should start when he is still a foal. There is much that can be done and a correct start at this age can make all the difference between a horse totally trusting the human race and not trusting it at all. A foal can be touched from the minute it is born, although this is often difficult if the mare is foal proud. Even the quietest of mares can become very protective and in such cases it is sensible to give her some time alone with her foal.

Simple lessons

Learning to lead is a lesson that can be taught a few days after birth. When starting to lead a foal two people are needed, one for the mare, the other for the foal. The foal should be led next to the mare, and gently encouraged forward by putting an arm around his quarters and gently pushing while keeping a tight hold on the foal slip.

In the next few months the foal should learn to lead from either side of the mare and to accept being led in front or further behind her. The foal soon learns to copy his dam, which can be extremely valuable when it comes to catching him. Whenever, you try to catch a foal you should always reward him when he comes straight away. The foal will then gain confidence in you and will eagerly await your call.

Once the youngster is used to human contact simple lessons can begin within the first year. He can be taught to pick up his feet in turn, and as he will not be too strong this should cause few problems. He will then easily accept the farrier rasping his feet at regular intervals when he attends the mare. The youngster can also be groomed with a soft brush, while someone else holds him; he should never be tied up at this age.

Stable manners

The horse is never too young to learn a few stable manners. Even if he is not stabled, he will benefit from being brought in each day and fed in the stable.

You should teach him to move over at your command and reinforce your verbal instruction by gently pushing him over with your hand. It is necessary that the horse learns to keep out of your way when required, to enable you to take care of his needs like mucking out and watering while he is still in the box.

The youngster should also respect you whenever you enter the stable, especially when carrying his feed. He should be made to wait until you have put his feed in the trough and retreated before he comes forward. Give the command 'Wait' in a strong tone and, if necessary, hold your hand up flat in front of you to indicate you require him to back off. This lesson is also useful when leading the horse from the box, as he will learn not to barge through the door when you tell him to wait.

Our aim is that by the time a youngster is weaned he should accept:

• Having the headcollar fitted without fuss.
• Having his feet picked up and attended to.
• Being groomed.
• Being led and being caught.

Tying up

There are two methods that can be used to tie a horse up for the first time. The first is used on older horses, whom you would not be able to hold should they play up; the second can be used on smaller, newly weaned foals who have less strength, and stamina.

Method 1
The area used to tie the horse up in for the first time should be uncluttered, and preferably have a soft surface. A tie-ring secured into a brick wall with grass underneath is ideal; otherwise a stable with a deep bed and high roof can be used. The

youngster should be fitted with a head-collar or halter that fits snugly. A strong lead rein should be attached to this, ensuring the clip faces down towards the horse's neck. The rope should be tied to the tie-ring using a quick-release knot. Contrary to normal practice, do not put a piece of breakable string between the tie-ring and the rope as this will only encourage the youngster to realize that if he pulls back he can free himself.

During this process the horse may put up a fight, and he should not be left unsupervised at any time, because the absence of the breakable string means that in an emergency he would not be able to free himself. Should the horse put up a fight

you can calm him with your voice, but do not get in the way or give him any titbits. The lesson is to accept being tied up without resistance, and he must learn that this is expected of him without compromise. Once the horse has learned the lesson of tying up, it is then safer to tie the rope on to a piece of strong, but breakable, bailing twine, attached to the ring.

Method 2
Fit the youngster with a snug headcollar as before, but to this you need to attach a long lunge rein. This method is best carried out in the stable with a good bed down. Ensure you are wearing gloves. Lead the youngster up to the tie-ring and

Fig. 93 To tolerate being tied up without pulling back is a lesson that must be learned.

pass the lunge rein through the ring until the slack is taken up. Talking to the youngster all the time, gradually move away from him, offering the voice commands to stand. He will probably want to follow you, and be ready because the minute he feels he is restrained he may try to pull away. Dig your heels in and simply hold fast. Do not jerk on the rein or pull on it. This method does require a battle of strengths, which is why it can only be used on a young foal, but in almost all cases, the foal soon gives in. The tie-ring provides you with an excellent lever against which to hold the rein. Once the foal accepts the restraint, you can move on to method one, the transition to which usually causes very few problems. However, do not use the breakable piece of string until you are sure the youngster accepts being tied up without pulling back.

Bitting

Bitting is the term used to describe putting a bit in the horse's mouth for the first time. It is a very important stage of training, as eventually it is the bit that will convey many of your wishes to the horse. A horse can be bitted as a yearling, and if he is being shown in-hand he will be expected to be exhibited in a bit. A snaffle bit is always used for early training and there are many different types in common use. A specially made mouthing bit which has 'keys' attached is often used. This is to encourage the horse to salivate and so accept the bit more readily. This type of bit is dispensed with once the horse starts work. An ordinary thick-jointed snaffle, usually with cheekpieces to prevent the bit from being pulled through the horse's mouth, can also be used from the start of

a horse's training. Whatever snaffle bit is decided upon it is vitally important that it is the correct size for the horse's mouth and that once in place it is adjusted properly. The bit should sit comfortably in the corners of the mouth, just wrinkling the lips slightly, without pulling on them. This is achieved by raising or lowering the cheekpieces as necessary.

The width of the bit is also very important. If it is too wide, the joint will fall too low in the mouth and may bang on the front teeth and possibly bruise the corners of the mouth. Such a bit will also allow the horse to put his tongue over it. If on the other hand the bit is too narrow it will pinch the corners of the mouth, which is not only uncomfortable for the horse, but will encourage him to lift his head to try to ease the pain and so evade the bit.

There are two ways of bitting for the first time. One is to fasten the bit to the headcollar; the other is to use the bridle straight away. When using a headcollar, the bit is fastened to the right side by a strap or piece of string. Then, standing with the horse's head over your shoulder, left hand holding the bit and right hand on the horse's nose, the bit is slipped into the horse's mouth and fastened on the left of the headcollar. The horse is encouraged to open his mouth and so take the bit by your sliding your thumb into the corner of his mouth. Before bitting for the first time it is often helpful to give the horse a piece of apple to ensure he has a moist mouth; and putting liquid molasses on the bit makes the whole thing a lot more pleasant.

The well-handled horse does not usually pose any problems at this stage and accepts the bit quite readily. The important thing is not to let him throw his head around, although he will inevitably try to raise it away from you. The whole process should be swift so that before the horse has time to think about what is going on the bit is securely in place.

If using the bridle from the start, you have extra leather to hold, but the process is the same. Stand in the same manner as described with headcollar bitting and hold the bridle cheekpieces in your right hand, resting on the horse's nose while keeping the head down. Then slip the bit in, swiftly put the headpiece over the horse's ears, and do up the throat-lash and noseband.

The disadvantage of using a bridle to begin with is that you have to slip it over the ears and fiddle with buckles. If your horse is at all headshy or a little nervous you should get him used to having a bridle put over his ears and noseband done up before attempting to bit him.

At all costs you should try to ensure that the horse does not become afraid and so start to throw his head around. This may result in the bit banging his teeth and a horse who subsequently resists being bitted in the future.

Once your horse has been bitted and is working on the lunge, or in long-reins (*see* Chapter 12) you may find that he will go better in one bit than another. However, do not be in a hurry to experiment with bits, unless the results you are getting with a particular bit are less than satisfactory.

Fig. 94 Bitting is a very important part of early training.

Usually, if a horse does not go well in a jointed snaffle it is worth trying a straight bar snaffle and vice-versa, rather than changing to another type of jointed snaffle. Rubber or mullen-mouth snaffles also offer an alternative, especially to a horse that is very sensitive. Once you have found a bit that suits your horse well, stick to it.

The roller

If your youngster has already been rugged up or accustomed to equipment at an early age then rollering will not be necessary, as he will already be used to the feel of something around his middle. If he has not then this is the next thing that he needs to accept before saddling. The roller/training surcingle should always have a pad beneath it to prevent any damage to the spine.

Rollering, like bitting, should pose few problems for the well-handled youngster. Start by showing the youngster the roller in your hands, let him sniff it and have a good look. Then fold the roller in half with the buckle end on top. Position yourself on the horse's near side, level with the withers. Gently position the roller in place behind the withers, making sure the horse knows it is there by rocking it gently backwards and forwards. Next, walk round to the horse's right side, unfold the roller and let the buckle end hang down. Walk back to his left side and gently reach under the horse's belly and take hold of the roller. Slowly bring it through to you and firmly buckle up the roller so that it is secure but not tight. Gauge your horse's reaction and allow him to accept the feel of the roller. Then gently tighten the roller one hole at a time until it is secure enough not to slip.

The horse will most likely accept the roller being fitted without making a fuss. It is when he moves and feels the pressure on his tummy that he might jump about, so be prepared. Walk him around the box, or school, then allow him to go loose for a few minutes. Once he appears to have accepted the roller, carefully remove it, making sure not to let the buckles bang on his legs. Repeat the exercise every day for a few days and frequently thereafter.

Rugging up

While rugging up is not a basic requirement to enable the horse to be started, it is another thing the horse needs to become accustomed to. More people are now appreciating that stabling horses, especially youngsters, is not the best way of keeping them in good health. It is because of the problems stabling causes, such as dust allergies which often result in Chronic Obstructive Pulmonary Disease (COPD), and the development of vices such as windsucking and weaving, that youngsters are far better off living out.

It therefore makes sense to accustom the horse to a rug at an early stage, so that he can be afforded more protection from harsh weather than a shelter alone can supply, yet still retain his freedom.

For the youngster that has been rollered, rugging is simply the next step. It is a sensible precaution, when rugging for the first time, to use an old lightweight sheet. It will be easy to manoeuvre, and will not be too great a loss if it should rip in the unlikely event that the horse tries to pull it off.

Have the rug prepared so that it is

125

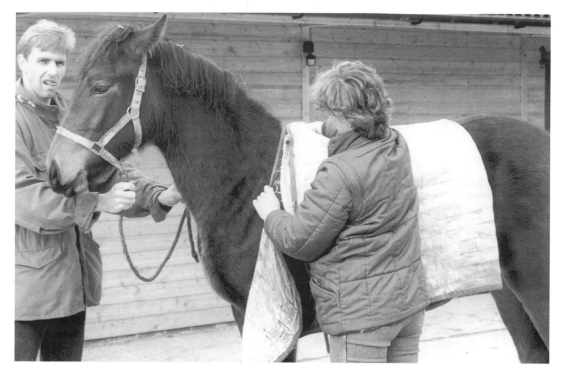

Fig. 95 Rugging up is something that the horse should be accustomed to at an early age, even if he is not to be rugged over the winter months.

folded from the back forwards. This will enable the rug to be placed over the horse's quarters with as little fuss as possible. Next show the horse the rug, letting him sniff and nuzzle it. Once he shows no signs of being wary of the rug gently place it, still folded, over his withers, making sure not to flap it about. Proceed slowly. Work from the front backwards: first do up the chest strap, then unfold the rug backwards until it is in place over the quarters. Put on the roller (an act the horse has already been accustomed to) and secure. Do not use a sheet with a fillet string at this stage as it may annoy the horse, or get caught up in the tail if you have to remove the rug quickly. Allow the horse some moments of freedom to get used to the feel

of it on him while walking round his box. It is a good idea put a bit in the horse's mouth first to give him something other than what you are doing to think about, or you can tie a haynet in front of the horse to place his attention elsewhere and to keep his head forward. If you bit the horse first, still attach the lead rope to the noseband, not the bit, and, as before, do not tie the horse up, but keep hold of the rope yourself.

Many big yards will advise against attempting such tasks on your own, but all of these preliminary requirements are fairly easily accomplished without help if you take your time. We have to bear in mind that in our favour we have a horse that is used to us and our voice, that trusts us and is in familiar surroundings. So we are already half-way to accomplishing these tasks. We are not under pressure to accomplish everything quickly and can take as long as the horse needs to accept one thing before moving on to another.

Routine

The horse is a creature of habit and once weaned a daily routine should be established to help him feel secure in his environment. A known routine will provide stability in the youngster's life, just as his mother did. Feed times should be regular, as should times of handling. However, it is a mistake to keep on handling the youngster; remember, he is still 'a baby' and, as such, his times of leisure and rest are extremely important to his development.

12 Educating the Young Horse

The system of punishment and reward becomes even more important as we move on to the horse's training up to the time he is ready for backing. As the youngster has learnt the basic requirements that will enable him to be handled safely there is little more we need to accomplish with him until he is a three-year-old. This does not mean we turn him out and forget about him, as we still need to repeat lessons regularly in order to establish understanding and respect. However, a time of turning away to allow the youngster to mature mentally and physically does no harm, especially if he has been shown in-hand.

Fig. 96 Repeating lessons over the winter months instils understanding and respect.

If you have bought, rather than bred, your own yearling you may find that he has had little handling and you will have to start his training from scratch. You will need to be a little more careful in your handling of him as he will be much bigger and much stronger. You should not aim to pick a fight with him: this is a great mistake as he will soon realize that he is stronger than you are. Take things slowly and you should find that you are able to make him obey your requests once he understands what you are asking. Rush it, and you will confuse him, resulting in his being unable to do what you ask of him simply because he doesn't understand.

ACCLIMATIZING TO TRAFFIC

You can introduce your youngster to traffic at this stage, but not until you are absolutely certain that you have full control of him. This means that he will obey your commands and that you take precautions such as putting a bridle on him and wearing gloves yourself. Many people feel it is vitally important that they introduce their youngster to traffic as soon as possible. I do not feel this is essential and in some cases it can be detrimental to the youngster's training. If he becomes frightened because he is too immature to accept the hustle and bustle of vehicles

Fig. 97 Introducing a horse to vehicles can be done gradually over the first few years, rather than weeks.

passing him, he will associate traffic with unpleasant experiences and you are then well on your way to producing a traffic-shy horse. The two- or three-year-old is usually more mature in his mental attitude and can concentrate for longer periods.

Start by taking your horse onto quiet lanes, preferably with an older 'nanny' horse. Wear a reflective tabard with the words 'Caution Young Horse', and thank motorists who slow down when passing. Once your horse accepts being led away from home and behaves well in quiet traffic then you can build up to slightly more busy roads; but never rush it – let your horse dictate the pace. If he seems quite happy then you are doing things right; if he is apprehensive then you are probably going faster than he would like.

Obviously in all situations you will have to take your horse's character into account. You should know him as an individual and if you notice him deviating from his normal behaviour then you should start to slow the pace a little.

PREPARING FOR BACKING

There are three main in-hand schooling methods which can be employed when starting (a term I prefer to 'breaking-in') your own horse. These are loose schooling, lungeing and long-reining. While each is an art in itself, becoming reasonably proficient at each – enough to educate a young horse in the basics at least – is not beyond the ability of any patient, attentive owner.

Many of you will have lunged a horse at some stage, but few of you may have long-reined or loose-schooled. Long-reining seems to carry a certain mystique, but in reality any sensible owner can learn the basic techniques in order to do it well. Loose-schooling is less accessible as few owners have the facilities to try it.

There is a natural progression between loose-schooling, lungeing and long-reining and one can benefit another if carried out at the appropriate stage of training.

I am often asked at what age you should start a youngster. There is no definite answer as every horse matures differently, and it is the level of maturity that dictates the pace. However, I would not start a horse before his third year, and between the autumn of his third year and the spring of his fourth year is usually about right. If you do not have any facilities you will have to take the weather into account because once started it is not advisable to stop and then have to start again.

Objectives

The most important ingredient at each stage of training is time. I cannot emphasize enough that each horse is an individual and each will progress at a different rate. We cannot therefore put a limit on the time it will take to complete any stage or on any one lesson before moving to the next.

However, whilst there are no timetables there are aims. We should consider the training of the young horse in terms of questions and answers, which are given as requests by us and responses by him. We start by asking very simple questions and must be prepared to wait for the horse to give the right answers. We ask the horse questions by the use of actions and verbal commands and we wait for the correct answers in the form of understanding and obedience. The horse who does not understand cannot obey and so patience is our most important asset.

Should the horse not give the right response, we must repeat our request until he does understand what is required of him. Each lesson should be clearly taught and not until the horse has thoroughly understood the lesson should he be asked anything new.

For the youngster just being started, lessons should be kept simple and short. As a guide approximately twenty minutes per lesson is long enough to start with. It is a misconception that making the horse continue until he has got it right is the best way. Instead of getting the desired result, this is only likely to confuse and tire him until it is impossible for him to respond in the desired way. It is far better to put the horse away after a short session and bring him out to try again later in the day after he has rested.

At this stage in our horse's education, whether we are loose-schooling, lungeing or long-reining, our basic aim is to have him going forward on command in a free and balanced outline. To accomplish our aims we must firstly relax our horse. Once we have succeeded to do this our task will be far easier as he will be more willing to listen to our requests and will try hard to carry them out.

Our goal at this stage is to produce a horse who will behave sensibly when it comes to backing.

Loose-schooling

Loose-schooling is particularly beneficial as a starting point. It will educate your horse to your voice commands and will allow him to become accustomed to your requests in a very natural way. Your horse will not immediately feel restricted by the use of tack and lunge reins, and his still maturing joints will not be subjected to unnecessary stresses and strains, often inadvertently caused by human restraint on the lunge. Once the horse is loose-schooling in a relaxed manner, he can be accustomed to the equipment that will be used for lungeing.

The aim of loose-schooling is to have the horse increasing or decreasing pace in a relaxed manner and in response to your voice, and body and whip position. the horse needs to be taught that if you position yourself behind him to a certain degree, you are wanting him to move forwards or increase his pace, depending on verbal commands also given. Conversely, if you position yourself on an angle slightly in front of him, you require him to slow his pace or stop, again aided by verbal commands.

Before you begin loose-schooling, introduce him to the whip. Let him see it before you start waving it about, otherwise he will be impossible to settle. All your movements in the loose school should be calm and encouraging the horse to move in the required direction without frightening him.

Lungeing

During loose-schooling your horse will have learned voice commands and will be used to you driving him forward around the school with the aid of the lungeing whip. Now we can progress to lungeing, which goes further in that you have more control over your horse. You can give him the 'feel' of being driven purposely from behind as with the rider's legs and seat, and to being restrained in front, as from the pressure the rider gives on the reins. This will develop him both mentally and physically, without having to put weight on his back.

Loose-schooling and lungeing can also be very beneficial when teaching the horse to jump later in his training.

Long-reining

Long-reining allows still more control over the horse. It is an excellent way of teaching the horse discipline without riding him. Without the distraction of a rider he can be taught simple aids, which he will later recognize in the riders legs and hands. Through the long reins, attached to the bit, the horse learns to respond to aids given through the rein. Through the contact of the long reins on his side, the horse learns the 'feel' of aids given on his sides through the rider's legs. Thus a horse that has been long-reined well is far more likely to respond quicker to a rider on his back when the time comes.

So, each method of training employed from the ground can progress from one stage to another and be structured to great benefit when it comes to backing and riding away. Through these schooling methods your horse will develop his muscles; he will become more supple, with increased joint flexion; and because he will learn to engage his hind legs more productively there will be an overall improvement in his balance and rhythm.

Fig. 98 Lungeing is the most accessible in-hand training method for most people and offers quite a lot of control over the horse.

Fig. 99 Long-reining allows even more control over the horse and is an excellent way of teaching discipline without riding him.

Loose-schooling, lungeing and long-reining are worthy of books in themselves, and since it is not possible to give full information here I would recommend reference to one of the excellent books that provides comprehensive guidance in these subjects.

BACKING

Once your horse is obedient on the lunge and/or long reins, and confident when being handled, he is ready to be backed. Most horses will be ready after about two months from first starting, but some will take longer. Only you can judge the exact moment.

Having had two months or so of training, your youngster will be physically stronger than before. However, having a rider on his back will force him to use muscles that he is not yet accustomed to using. This is why backing should be done gradually and gently. You might think that your well-mannered horse will pose no problems, but even the quietest of horses can become apprehensive when first mounted, so you need to give him time to become accustomed to your weight and movements on his back.

Backing is the act of mounting for the first time and no riding, as such, is involved. You will need extreme patience and should be satisfied with small accomplishments at first. Rushing only makes

133

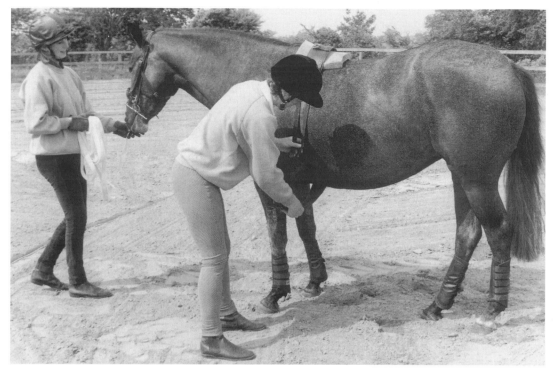

Fig. 100 Once your horse is obedient on the lunge and / or long-reins he is ready to be backed.

the horse worried and anxious, which can cause problems when it comes to riding away.

Who Should Back Him?

This is a question that often causes much debate. Some people feel that the person who has trained him so far should not be the one to back him, as he will need to give reassurance from the ground. Remember how important the voice is, and how quickly horses come to trust a familiar voice. Others believe that only a light-weight rider should back the horse, even if the horse is big and well matured.

Personally, I feel the person to back the

horse for the first time is the one who is quite happy and confident about doing so. It is no good using a rider simply because he is light, as he may have no experience and the horse will be the first to sense fear. Similarly, it is pointless to back the horse yourself unless you have no qualms about doing so. While few well-prepared horses actually 'put up a show,' an apprehensive rider may cause a change of character resulting in unnecessary bad behaviour from your otherwise sensible horse.

The minimum manpower required to back a horse is two people – the handler and the rider – and each has clearly defined responsibilities. These should be made clear before starting to avoid confusion at a crucial moment. The handler is

Fig. 101 As soon as the rider is in place the horse should be led off onto the track.

responsible for controlling the horse and the rider for simply staying put! The rider must not attempt to control the horse in any way, and must endeavour to stay on whatever happens. If the horse plays up and manages to unseat his rider, he will have learnt that in behaving badly it is a fairly simple matter to rid himself of his rider whenever he feels like it.

Final preparation

To ensure the day of backing goes smoothly there are things you can do to prepare the horse. Firstly, when backing, the horse will experience a person higher than himself for the first time. This can be a little worrying to him, so getting him used to seeing someone higher than himself is not a bad idea. You can teach him to walk up to the mounting block and to stand still. Then stand on the block and lean towards him, but do not lean over him. Repeat this lesson until he is quite happy about seeing you there.

To get him used to the noise of the saddle you can slap it and rock it gently back and forth. You can also put pressure in the stirrups by pushing down on them. Lungeing with the stirrups down will also get him used to the feel of something next to his sides. These simple lessons will only take a few extra minutes each day,

135

but will pay dividends when backing for real.

Some people back a horse in the stable because they feel the confined space prevents any thought in the horse's mind of trying to get free. I prefer not to do this because if the horse does anything silly the confined space can actually make things more difficult. The handler could get squashed against the wall and the person mounting could get squashed on the ceiling! Some people also use a mounting block to mount for the first time. Again I prefer not to as the horse can easily bang against it, or the handler may trip over it if the horse suddenly lurches away. I prefer to take the horse to his normal working area, which he already associates with obedience to training requests.

Tack your horse up as for lungeing, with the stirrups removed, and walk him to the working area. Then lunge him on both reins as normal.

Leaning over the withers

Bring him into the middle of the school and halt him squarely. If you are handling, gather up the lunge rein and take hold of the horse, talking in a soothing manner, while the rider puts pressure on the saddle with his or her arms.

Still holding the horse by the lunge rein, the handler should face the horse's shoulder and smoothly give the rider a leg up until he is lying over the saddle. The rider should then stroke the horse while the handler offers him a carrot or a few nuts. The rider then slips back down to the floor, makes much of him, and the process is repeated again a few times. In most

cases the horse is so pleased to be getting a treat, he takes very little notice of the whole event.

It will depend on each individual horse whether any more can be done at this stage. If the horse seems to accept the rider then the procedure can be repeated on the horse's right side. If the horse seems a little nervous it would be wiser to put him away and have another session later in the day. There is no benefit in rushing at this stage, and it is wise to allow the horse to dictate the pace. You should be perceptive to your horse's state of mind and choose the most appropriate course of action.

Staying up

It will depend on the individual horse how quickly things progress from here. However, it is wise to take a few days of repeating previous lessons just to make sure the horse totally accepts what is happening before moving on. You should not aim to do things so quickly that the horse is given no time to think, otherwise the horse may rebel later on.

Once your horse has accepted the rider lying over his back, he can be walked around with the rider in this position. Horses very rarely react to having weight on their backs whilst standing still and if there is to be any reaction, it is most likely to come when the horse is moved. Therefore, when first moving off with the rider lying over the horse's back be prepared for a reaction, and if it comes halt the horse immediately. Then repeat the process once more until the horse is walking around calmly.

Next the rider should slip his right leg over the saddle and gently sit in place, although leaning forward so as not to startle the horse. Gradually the rider should sit up and pat the horse, offering soothing words the whole time. Again this must be repeated a few times. The rider should then dismount with the same caution and the stirrups put back in place.

The next lesson will see the rider mounted and being led. Having been given a leg up in the same way, the rider should put both feet into the stirrups. When mounted and being led for the first time, it is essential the rider does not fall off, so the stirrups are used to provide security and to help balance. As soon as the rider is in place lead the horse off onto the track. Again, you should both be ready in case

the horse gives any reaction. However, if backing is done smoothly it is unlikely that you will receive any surprises. The rider assumes a totally passive role, and is in fact simply a passenger at this stage. He or she follows the horse's movements, but does not give any aids.

Once your horse has walked a little way, halt and make much of him. Then walk on again, halt and reward him again. Repeat this on both reins.

Within a few days you will be able to begin lungeing your horse with a rider on top. Start by keeping him on a short lunge line and simply walk and halt as before. The rider is still a passenger at this stage and does not give leg aids or use the reins.

Fig. 102 Within a few days, lungeing when ridden can commence.

Fig. 103 Having backed your horse you should simply repeat and confirm each lesson, making much of him when he conforms to your requests.

Trotting

Once the horse is accustomed to walking with a rider on his back on the lunge, trotting can commence. The rider should at this point take hold of the reins. Although the control of the horse still rests with the person lungeing, the rider may need to use the reins to keep the horse's head up. If allowed to put their heads down towards their front legs some horses will try to buck. However it is important that the rider does not yank on the reins or make any other sudden movements.

When trotting, the rider should always rise to the trot, so as not to put undue strain on the horse's back. The rider must keep his weight forward and sit as lightly as possible in the saddle.

The worst thing most horses try to do at this stage is give a buck, so both you and the rider must try to anticipate this. With a young horse this is not too difficult. He will try to get his head down and arch his back, an action that is immediately apparent. Before the horse has accomplished this both handler and rider should have recognized the signs. Immediately send the horse on into a more active trot, flicking the lungeing whip if necessary. The rider should at the same time give the voice command 'Tr-rot' to divert the horse's attention and prevent the buck being carried out.

PRACTICE

Having backed your horse, you should simply repeat and confirm what you have

138

so far taught him. During his short ridden sessions, he is mounted and dismounted regularly from both sides, he learns to stand still when being backed, and is walked and trotted on both reins. He should not do any work in canter as he is still too immature for this to serve any purpose; by doing so you risk his tripping and falling.

In order not to confuse the horse you must allow him time to become used to the rider's weight and movement on his back before expecting him to learn the use of the rider's aids. This reaffirming process continues for a couple of weeks.

When first carrying the weight of a rider your horse will tire easily, so sessions need to be built up gradually. You should stick to the principle of keeping your horse's work varied, so some days he will be lunged and ridden for a short time, while on other days he might be long-reined and not ridden at all, and on another day he might be loose-schooled and then ridden.

Once the horse is sensible when being ridden in the work area he can be walked out on quiet roads. An older 'nanny' horse will be of great benefit when first hacking out. He is less likely to spook at silly things and will be well behaved in traffic, an example we hope our youngster will soon learn to follow.

TURNING AWAY

Once backed, there is little more the young horse can learn at this stage. If you aim to

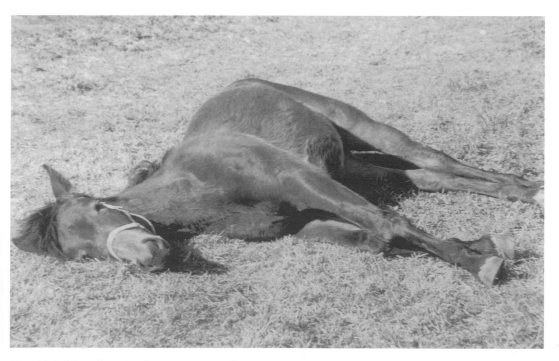

Fig. 104 After the initial training period your youngster can be turned away to mature both physically and mentally.

go straight into the second elementary stage of ridden work you risk mental and physical damage to your horse. Therefore, for about six weeks after first backing you should not attempt to teach anything new, merely carry on reinforcing the ridden, lungeing, loose-schooling and long-reining lessons, which have been previously carried out.

At the end of this period it is hoped that you will have established a sound level of communication with your horse based on trust. If you have done the job well he should be a confident and sensible youngster, who is sufficiently balanced when working both ridden and unridden. He can now be turned away for a time to allow him to mature both physically and mentally, before the second stage of more serious schooling work commences. If your youngster was started in the spring of his third year he will probably be strong and developed enough to come back into work in the autumn. However, it is not unusual to leave less well-developed youngsters until the spring of their fourth year.

The whole aim is to produce a willing and confident partner. Once we have this, we can progress into any area we choose, gaining immense satisfaction along the way.

EXPECTATIONS FOR THE YOUNG HORSE

As described throughout this chapter, the starting process and basic education of all young horses is the same, no matter what sphere we hope they are destined for. It becomes clear that only when the horse has been schooled enough to demonstrate his natural abilities can he be taken on to a specific area of training, perhaps show jumping or dressage for example. The decision on what to do next with your horse once you have started him can be a difficult one, especially if you have definite plans to compete in a certain competitive discipline. What happens if your horse simply does not have enough ability? Or what if he has so much talent that you, as his rider, will not be able to do him justice? Every horse is an individual, as is every rider. If having bred and trained your own horse you do 'click' as a partnership, you will find it very difficult ever to replace the special relationship that you will enjoy for many years to come. However, if as a team you simply do not live up to expectations, you may have to take the decision to find your young horse a new home. And what then? Well, you could always start all over again, and repeat the experience with a new foal!

Index